Psychotic Children Grown Up

A Prospective Follow-Up Study in Adolescence and Adulthood

Special Issue of ISSUES IN CHILD MENTAL HEALTH
A Journal of Psychosocial Process

William Goldfarb
Donald Meyers
Judy Florsheim
Nathan Goldfarb

HUMAN SCIENCES PRESS
72 Fifth Avenue   3 Henrietta Street
NEW YORK, NY 10011 ● LONDON, WC2E 8LU

Library of Congress Catalog Number 77-93594
ISBN: 0-87705-331-6
Copyright 1978 by Human Sciences Press

HUMAN SCIENCES PRESS
72 Fifth Avenue
New York, New York 10011

Printed in the United States of America

Vol. 5, No. 2   *Spring/Summer 1978*

ISSUES IN CHILD MENTAL HEALTH: A JOURNAL OF PSYCHOSOCIAL PROCESS

Foreword   105
        E. James Anthony, M.D.

Psychotic Children Grown Up - A Prospective Follow-Up
   Study in Adolescence and Adulthood   108
        William Goldfarb, M.D., Ph.D.
        Donald I. Meyers, M.D.
        Judy Florsheim, M.S.
        Nathan Goldfarb, Ph.D.

Discussion: The Outcome of Infantile Psychosis   173
        Leon Eisenberg, M.D.

Index   181

ISSUES IN CHILD MENTAL HEALTH: A JOURNAL OF PSYCHOSOCIAL PROCESS, is sponsored by the Jewish Board of Family and Children's Services, one of the largest social agencies in the country and is unique in offering the yield of experience of an interdisciplinary staff of psychologists, psychoanalysts, social workers, educators, sociologists, nurses, anthropologists, language specialists, child care workers, and health care administrators as they work together in a blend of service training and research to find new ways of helping emotionally disturbed children.

MANUSCRIPTS, preferably not longer than 20 pages, shoud be sent in triplicate to Donald I. Meyers, Editor, 4560 Delafield Ave., Bronx, N.Y. 10471. The entire manuscript should be double-spaced and should be typed using a 70 character line. Manuscripts should conform to the style indicated in the Publication Manual of the American Psychological Association. The full name, address and affiliation of each author should appear on the title page.

SUBSCRIPTIONS are on a per-volume basis, $20 per volume for institutions, $10 for individuals. Orders should be addressed to the business office. Overseas subscriptions should be addressed to Human Sciences Press, 3 Henrietta Street, London, WC2E 8LU England. Foreign subscriptions are an additional $2.

ADVERTISING inquiries should be made to Stan Goldstein at the business office.

BUSINESS OFFICE: Human Sciences Press, 72 Fifth Avenue, New York, N.Y. 10011.

INDEXED in Community Mental Health Review, Current Literature/Social Work in Health Care. Public Health Reviews, Chicorel Abstracts to Reading and Learning Disabilities.

ISSN 0362-403X   LC 76-21890   ICMHDI 5(2) 101-183(1978)

FOREWORD

E. James Anthony, M.D.*

In reading through this prospective follow-up study of psychotic children, one is struck by several features at once—the clarity of the exposition, the logical development of the research argument, the freedom from preconceived notions, the careful delineation of the sample under investigation and the derivation of outcome criteria from systematically made observations over time—all serve to remind us of the cautionary Hippocratic precept:

"In medicine one must pay attention not to plausible theorizing but to experience and reason together. I agree that theorizing is to be approved, provided that it is based on facts, and systematically makes its deductions from what is observed. But conclusions drawn from unaided reason can hardly be serviceable; only those drawn from observable fact."

The facts that have been accumulated by the investigators are used with elegant economy to support the main thrust of the inquiry—the value of prognostic elements contained in the earlier part of the study. The facts also furnish patterns of change in the social adaptation of the subjects and this, in my opinion, is one of the major contributions of the work. There is no question in my mind, speaking as a prospectively-oriented researcher, that the "follow along" type of investigation has many distinctive advantages over the follow back and the simply designed before-and-after follow-up procedures. The retrospective method is fraught with distortion while the two-step forward investigation tends to leave an unknowable vacuum haunted by intermediate variables. In the prospective mode, contact is maintained with the sample during the

*Dr. Anthony is the Blanche F. Ittleson Professor of Child Psychiatry and Director of the Eliot Division of Child Psychiatry at the Washington University School of Medicine, St. Louis, Missouri.

interim period between assessments and thus systematic observation continues to enrich the data pool from which the assessors draw their conclusions and make their ratings.

I would like to draw attention to what I regard as another major strength of the study. In these more sophisticated days, it is fast becoming a truism that the individual's adjustment is a function both of his own capacities as well as the capacities of his social environment to meet his needs. Quite rightly, in my opinion, the Ittleson group have avoided some of the pitfalls that have plagued other studies: they have not, for example, been led astray by nosological labels that vary from decade to decade; they have not taken for granted the debatable inference that the child psychotic is father to the adult one; and they have not accepted the narrower clinical dictum that the proper study of mankind is pathology. All of us in this field and in neighboring fields are fast realizing the need to consider the human individual, both child and adult, in terms of adaptive competence and all of us are finding, to our pleased surprise, that global psychiatric appraisals of adaptive functioning that assay a wide variety of responses in the areas of communication, relationship, cognition, sociability, educability and self-care, offer us the best assessment of this factor. One should acknowledge, in passing, that this viewpoint owes much to the assiduous work of Leopold Bellak who has long claimed that the study of the basic ego functions brings some degree of order into an otherwise heterogeneous collection of clinical groupings based on symptomatic behavior. Bellak sees the psychoses as *quantitative* variations of adaptive functioning and considers that the various types have as their only common denominator this overall poor adaptive capacity of the ego. Of course, behind the ego functions lies the degree of integrity of the nervous system and the Ittleson investigators are well aware of this in their separation of the sample into neurologically and environmentally determined subgroups. To make a dichotomy of this kind requires a special sensitivity to neurophysiological functioning together with an equally sensitive appreciation of the individual's psychology and his psychosocial environment. The emphasis on environment is especially significant since it is often totally overlooked or taken for granted.

What is innovative in this study (and will, I predict, have a methodological impact on future prospective research until the so-called "path analysis" becomes more manageable) is the classification of each child's longitudinal course in terms of profiles or patterns of change derived from criteria of normalcy based on psychiatric ratings of ego and on placement course. One is so habituated to looking at the child psychotic frozen in time that we are only too apt to forget that under helpful conditions of living, he too can move forward and into a normal channel of development where he can exercise "an ordinary expectable degree of autonomy." I was impressed and rendered much more hopeful than I have been for years by the improvements registered in the study, the relationship of this improvement to the global ego and its environment, the maintenance and continuation of improvement in a large number following discharge from treatment, and the influence on the pathway to better health by the presence or absence of neurological dysfunction. It is of interest that the nonorganic group not only tended to respond better to treatment but, at the same time, they were more vulnerable than their "organic" counterparts to psychotic decompensations.

Altogether, this publication may help to inject a new optimism into a field in which earlier, the diagnosis of childhood psychosis has been generally regarded as tantamount to a condemnation to a lifelong incompetence; the therapeutic successes of Bettelheim, Deslauriers and some others, because of the lack of rigor in the respective studies, have regretfully generated more skepticism than scientific acceptance. The Ittleson Monograph should help to counteract much of this and inculcate a greater spirit of clinical optimism. The senior investigators have kept their own therapeutic biases well under control allowing themselves only the very tentative comment that "The curative role of psychotherapy in early childhood psychosis still awaits carefully controlled evaluation."

I must put in a final word about the setting in which all this excellent work is carried out day in and day out, year in and year out, as the decades pass. The Henry Ittleson Center for Child Research in New York has made a name for itself not only because it has provided Goldfarb and Meyers and their colleagues with an almost ideal center for the longitudinal investigation of severe pathology in children but, at the same time, it has provided the children with a comprehensive program of treatment that has consistently been conducted with a high degree of professional proficiency. The Ittleson Foundation, the National Institute of Mental Health, the William T. Grant Foundation and the Ehrmann Foundation must be jointly congratulated on their wisdom in maintaining this outstanding center that has enabled the world at large to reorient itself and its thinking to this enigmatic disorder. I wish the investigators an equally productive outcome in their next ten years of study.

PSYCHOTIC CHILDREN GROWN UP- A PROSPECTIVE FOLLOW-UP STUDY IN ADOLESCENCE AND ADULTHOOD

William Goldfarb, M.D., Ph.D.
Donald I. Meyers, M.D.
Judy Florsheim, M.S.
Nathan Goldfarb, Ph.D.*

Follow-up studies of psychotic children who have been observed and treated early in life are necessary to increase our knowledge of their life course and to cast light on factors contributing to the vicissitudes and episodic variations of their emotional and social responses. They enable us to observe individual differences in life course and to witness the development and changes of the adaptive disorders uniquely characteristic of children with early childhood psychosis. Finally, they clarify the links between early childhood psychoses and adult psychoses.

There have been many follow-up studies of these children by most of the larger clinical installations and by clinical investigators in this country and abroad (Annell, 1963; Bartak & Rutter, 1976; Bender, 1970;

---

*Dr. William Goldfarb is Director of the Henry Ittleson Center for Child Research, a division of the Jewish Board of Family and Children's Services; and Clinical Professor of Psychiatry, College of Physicians and Surgeons, Columbia University. He is also a faculty member of the Columbia University Psychoanalytic Center for Training and Research. Dr. Donald I. Meyers is Director of Experimental Psychiatry at the Henry Ittleson Center for Child Research; and Associate Clinical Professor of Psychiatry, College of Physicians and Surgeons, Columbia University. He is also chairman of the Child Analysis Training Program and a Training and Supervising Analyst at the Columbia University Psychoanalytic Center for Training and Research. Mrs. Judy Florsheim is Research Psychologist at the Henry Ittleson Center for Child Research. Dr. Nathan Goldfarb is Statistical Consultant at the Henry Ittleson Center for Child Research and Professor of Statistics and Administration, Hofstra University.

A Publication of the Childhood Schizophrenia Project of the Henry Ittleson Center for Child Research under support of the Ittleson Family Foundation, the National Institute of Mental Health Grant No. 2 RO 1 MH05753-13, the William T. Grant Foundation and the Herman A. and Amelia Ehrmann Foundation.

Bender & Grugett, 1956; Bennett & Klein, 1966; Bettelheim, 1967; Brown, 1960, 1963; Colbert & Koegler, 1961; Creak, 1963; Davids, Ryan, & Salvatore, 1968; DeMyer, Barton, DeMyer, Norton, Allen, & Steele, 1973; DeMyer, Barton, Alpern, Kimberlin, Allen, Yank, & Steele, 1974; Eaton, & Menascolino, 1966; Eisenberg, 1956, 1957; Fish, Shapiro, Campbell, & Wile, 1968; Freedman & Bender, 1957; Goldfarb, 1970, 1974; Kaufman, Frank, Friend, Heims, & Weiss, 1962; Lotter, 1974 a&b; Menascolino, 1965; Reiser & Brown, 1964; Rutter, 1965; Rutter, Greenfield, & Lockyer, 1967). However, it is difficult to integrate these findings inasmuch as diagnoses have differed, samples of children have undoubtedly represented different populations and appraisal techniques have varied. There is still need for study of outcome in early childhood psychosis; and, undoubtedly, precise definitions of the samples, classifications and appraisal procedures will have to be specified in order to facilitate the integration of the findings of different observers.

Most of the studies of outcome have depended on retrospective recall and existing records; and the children often have been studied long after leaving the treating installation. Significant details of development and factors influencing their developmental characteristics have often, therefore, not been available. This informational ambiguity limits the validity of evaluations of outcome. Linked to the doubtful validity of appraisals based on retrospective data has been the tendency to define outcomes merely in terms of adult nomenclature while losing the thread between the adult conditions and the earlier developmental influences. The latter limitations are represented, for example, in Bender and Grugett's report (1956) that 85% of diagnosed schizophrenic children were later diagnosed as schizophrenic in adolescence and adulthood. The same limitations are to be noted in Bennett and Klein's follow-up (1966) of 14 schizophrenic children 30 years after observation in childhood. Of present interest, those nine who were located in state hospitals on follow-up could not be differentiated from deteriorated adult schizophrenia patients, though their entire life course, and certainly their childhood, differed from that of most adult schizophrenics.

The most productive approach to appraisal is one which emphasizes adaptive competence, which in turn embodies ultimate social outcomes (including educational and vocational). Several investigators who have studied social outcomes have been able to define some early factors associated with these outcomes. In his study of 63 autistic children, for example, Eisenberg (1956) noted that the presence or absence of language by age five differentiated two groups of autistic children. Of the thirty children without effective speech by age five, only one attained marginal adjustment and he was eventually hospitalized. In contrast, about half the children with language at age five showed fair to good adolescent adjustment. Later, in 1965, Rutter studied 64 cases and demonstrated significant correlations between social outcome and such dimensions as IQ, speech, severity of disorder, and schooling. Response to intelligence testing was the most important single variable associated with outcome. The great majority of the "poor" outcome cases (75%) and "very poor" outcome cases (85%) had IQs below 60. In anticipation of the present investigation based on a larger sample of children with more extended follow-up observation, our own study of 48 psychotic children discharged between 1953 and 1963 strongly supported the association of language, IQ, and global adaptive status, with adjustment at discharge from treatment at 9½ years of age and with follow-up adjustment at 16½ years of age (1970). In his recent study of social outcomes in autistic children, Lotter (1974) noted a positive correlation of social outcome with speech, intelligence quotient (IQ), social quotient (SQ), severity of disorder, milestones, sex, convulsions and EEG, and years of schooling. There were no significant correlations with birth weight, perinatal complications, age of onset, social class and family mental illness.

It will be noted that these follow-up studies have quite consistently confirmed the predictive power of certain specific attributes in the child himself. As measured, these attributes are largely overlapping or intercorrelated expressions of residual adaptive capacity. We have demonstrated positive association, for example, among such operationally defined measures as ego status, speech and communication levels, response to intelligence testing, psychomotor ability, educational attainment and many others as well (Goldfarb, 1961, 1970, 1974). Thus, as will be seen, in appraising the social and clinical status of each child, we have preferred in this study to employ global psychiatric appraisals of adaptive functioning which embodied assays of relational response, speech and language, receptor response, cognition, social maturity and self care, and educational responsiveness. We have recorded the strong predictive power of these summed ratings of ego status (Goldfarb, 1970).

Lotter (1974) has emphasized the role of sex; and he has noted consistently poorer outcome among the girls in his psychotic population. We too have noted the lower mean ratings of adaptive status (e.g. IQ, language level) among the girls (Goldfarb, 1974). However, we have pointed out that the boys and girls have not differed in outcome as reflected in global ego status when matched for neurological status and ego status at initiation of residential treatment (Goldfarb, 1970). Certainly, the notion that psychotic girls, in contrast to psychotic boys, have a uniformly bad prognosis has been contradicted by our studies.

In our own work, neurological integrity of the psychotic child has been significantly linked to response to residential treatment; but it has not been significantly associated with outcome in later follow-up after discharge from the treating residence (Goldfarb, 1970).

In contrast to the predictive strength of measures of the child's primary adaptive capacity (ego status, IQ, SQ, language), the role of influences outside the child and residing in his social environment have been less well established. Perhaps it is more accurate to say these factors have not been sufficiently studied. Here we refer to socio-economic position of the family, and psychosocial functioning of the family. Lotter (1974) has noted that all (n = 4) of his good outcome cases come from intact middle class families and all (n = 5) of his fair outcome cases come from working class families. These represent very small samples of children. Nor have our own data confirmed the class trends reported by Lotter. In fact, in one comprehensive longitudinal study of psychotic children during inpatient treatment, there was an inverse relationship between family socio-economic position and measures of capacity of the children, so that lower class psychotic children were higher in capacity than upper class children at the beginning and end of three years of residential treatment (Goldfarb, 1974). We shall be testing the predictive correlations between family social class and outcomes in the present study.

In considering educational and therapeutic influences on childhood psychosis, the advantageous effects of amount of schooling have also been noted, perhaps not convincingly since the highest ordered child is likely to receive more education (Eisenberg, 1956; Rutter, 1965). Aside from Kaufman and his colleagues (1962), the tendency has been to deny the specific merits of psychotherapy. While a control of untreated psychotic children has been lacking at the Ittleson Center, we have had the strong conviction, drawn from the extensive management of psychotic children and intensive treatment of individual psychotic children, that comprehensive treatment does enhance the psychotic child's forward progress. For example, we have reported the excellent educational progress of psychotic children once they are placed in residential treatment, and provided they possess the cognitive competence normally required for educational progress (Goldfarb & Pollack, 1964). Similarly, we have reported that a residential program seemed to be superior to day treatment for psychotic children who are free of neurological deficits and have been reared in severely disturbed families and that this difference did not apply to children with neurological deficits (Goldfarb, Goldfarb & Pollack, 1966). Even so, however, the curative role of psychotherapy in early childhood psychosis still awaits carefully controlled evaluation.

THE PRESENT INVESTIGATION

The objectives of the present report are simple. In the first place, it proposes to describe social and psychiatric outcomes in adolescence and adulthood of a group of psychotic children who had been treated in early school age in the residential treatment program of the Ittleson Center for Child Research between 1953 and 1969. In this regard it is a long term follow-up study in which the same children were observed for many years from early childhood to maturity. In the second place, the report proposes to summarize the association between selected independent variables and psychiatric and social outcomes in maturity in these children. Because we are finally able to assay outcomes in adolescence and early adult maturity, it is now possible to formulate several prognostic paradigms which we shall certainly want to test out prospectively with a new group of psychotic children.

The investigation is a prospective one in that each child became a member of the study sample on admission to residential treatment and was subsequently studied and reported continuously and systematically while in therapy and after discharge from the residence. The children and families were informed from the start as to the research as well as therapeutic intent of the Center; and, in general, they were accepting of the regular annual psychiatric appraisals of ego functioning while in the residence and the biennial psychiatric appraisals after discharge. The validity of these psychiatric assays was enhanced by the in-depth information provided by the comprehensive therapeutic program of the residence and the systematic and structured assays of the research program, including psychological and language testing. The rather intensive and continuing contact with the children and families was further facilitated on discharge from the residence by an after-care program in which the research psychiatrist played an active participant role. Aside from the unique validity of such therapeutically rooted data, the regular, serial accumulation of clinical information recorded in a structured fashion enabled analysis of changes at key points in the histories of the children. Thus it has been possible to evaluate psychiatric and social adjustment at admission to residential treatment, at discharge from residential treatment and at various points in longitudinal follow-up after discharge.

The observational data to be reported have been gathered by a research psychiatrist (D.I.M.), associated with the investigation from the very beginning. Every subject was seen individually for systematic psychiatric study by the psychiatrist who used the method of clinical interview as the basis of psychiatric diagnosis and for assay of ego status at each point in follow-up. Supporting information regarding the subjects' social and educational adjustment was obtained by the psychiatrist through interview of parents. In the case of institutional placement during the follow-up phase, additional information regarding the social and educational adjustment of the children was obtained from caretaking personnel and from case records. The psychiatrist also had access to information regarding children's adjustment obtained by the after care social worker[1] who had ongoing contact with the families and with educational, psychiatric, and social agencies with whom the children were involved during the follow-up phase.

THE DIAGNOSIS OF EARLY CHILDHOOD PSYCHOSIS

A primary factor determining each child's admission to the Ittleson Center was his presenting diagnosis and classification as psychotic. In every instance, a child was admitted to the study population if two child psychiatrists agreed on their independently made diagnoses. The gathering of the present sampling of children and their observation took place over almost 20 years. As might be expected, during this long period there were some shifts in terminology and classification. However, we are persuaded that these shifts, reflecting increasingly precise diagnostic criteria, have not altered the diagnostic character of our sample of children. Between 1953 and 1961, all the children were considered to be manifesting the schizophrenic syndrome of childhood. Diagnoses at that time employed the criteria for the diagnosis of childhood schizophrenia elaborated by Potter (1933), Bender (1941), Kanner (1943, 1949) and Mahler (1952). In 1961 we determined that all the diagnostic criteria which had been employed till then could be subsumed in the nine diagnostic criteria recommended by the British Working Party for diagnosis of the schizophrenic syndrome of childhood (Creak, 1961). Since 1961, we have employed these criteria for diagnosis of early childhood psychosis.

---

[1]Mrs. Gwen Zeichner

These criteria* are as follows:

1. *Gross and sustained impairment of emotional relationships* with people. This includes the more usual aloofness and the empty clinging (so-called symbiosis), also abnormal behavior towards other people as persons, such as using them impersonally. Difficulty in mixing and playing with other children is often outstanding and long-lasting.

2. *Apparent unawareness of own personal identity* to a degree inappropriate to age. This may be seen in abnormal behavior towards himself, such as posturing or exploration and scrutiny of parts of his body. Repeated self-directed aggression, sometimes resulting in actual damage, may be another aspect of his lack of integration (see also point 5) as is also the confusion of personal pronouns (see point 7).

3. *Pathological preoccupation with particular objects* or certain characteristics of them without regard to their accepted functions.

4. *Sustained resistance to change in the environment* and a striving to maintain or restore sameness. In some instances behavior appears to aim at producing a state of perceptual monotony.

5. *Abnormal perceptual experience* (in the absence of discernible organic abnormality) is implied by excessive, diminished, or unpredictable response to sensory stimuli—for example, visual and auditory avoidance (see also points 2 and 4), insensitivity to pain and temperature.

6. Acute, excessive, and seemingly illogical *anxiety* is a frequent phenomenon. This tends to be precipitated by change, whether in material environment or in routine, as well as by temporary interruption of a symbiotic attachment to persons or things (compare points 3 and 4, and also 1 and 2). (Apparently commonplace phenomena or objects tend to become invested with terrifying qualities. On the other hand, an appropriate sense of fear in the face of real danger may be lacking.)

---

*Signs 1, 2, 6 and 7 have been found in every child in a sample of 48 children diagnosed at Ittleson Center (Goldfarb, 1970).

7. *Speech* may have been lost or never acquired, or may have failed to develop beyond a level appropriate to an earlier stage. There may be confusion of personal pronouns (see point 2), echolalia, or other mannerisms of use and diction. Though words or phrases may be uttered, they may convey no sense of ordinary communication.

8. *Distortion in motility patterns*—for example, (a) excess as in hyperkinesis, (b) immobility as in catatonia, (c) bizarre postures, or ritualistic mannerisms, such as rocking and spinning (themselves or objects).

9. A background of serious *retardation* in which islets of normal, near normal, or exceptional intellectual function or skill may appear.

In recent years there has been an increasing practice to reserve the term "schizophrenia" for children with onset of psychosis after seven years of age; and to reserve the term "autism" for children with onset in the first two years of the characteristic symptoms described by Kanner. All children in the present study showed developmental disorders in the first two years of life. However, they have seemed to be more diverse in phenomenology and competence than implied in a strict application of Kanner's criteria so that we now designate the children who meet the British criteria instances of early childhood psychosis.

Primary autistic manifestations were noted in children at all levels of adaptive competence. However, clear-cut cases of infantile autism with most patent and indisputable expressions of human withdrawal, compulsive, stereotypic, ritualistic behavior, and impairments in communication were particularly noteworthy in the present group in children at lowest levels of intellectual and ego competence. (As will be described in the tables to follow, these children have been classified at lowest ego levels 1 and 2).

INTAKE CRITERIA

The application of a similar set of diagnostic criteria by other psychiatric observers assures a degree of overlap in the diverse samples of early childhood psychosis observed at different clinics. However, we have also been impressed by obvious differences among these samples of psychotic children. Such differences may even occur over time within the same treatment installation. The specific character of each research sample thus needs to be spelled out carefully. While a commonly accepted system of diagnostic classification assures overlap among different samples of psychotic children, the unique attributes of each sample are strongly influenced also by relevant intake practices. Thus psychotic children admitted at an early age have been shown to be different in numerous ways from those admitted at an older age (Goldfarb, 1974). Differences in longitudinal patterns between psychotic children with normal IQs and those with retarded levels of functioning have also been demonstrated (Goldfarb, 1974; Bartak & Rutter, 1976). We have noted sampling differences between psychotic children from poor homes and those from upper class homes (Goldfarb, 1974). It is thus useful to define the intake criteria regulating the flow of children into the Ittleson Center.

Following are the specific intake practices which have undoubtedly influenced the sampling of psychotic children studied at the Ittleson Center:

1. Admission at early school age—approximately five to nine years of age. They tended to concentrate at an age when children were beginning formal education in the first grade.

The decision to offer care and service to psychotic children of early school age undoubtedly influenced the character of our research sample. The population included many children who had extensive professional attention very early in the pre-school period. However, it also included some children who had evidenced developmental difficulties in infancy but whose emotional, intellectual and social difficulties became most troublesome to the families and community only when the children were faced with the special challenges of the early school years. We would propose that this selective influence would tend to make the present research sample more heterogenous than a group of children treated for childhood psychosis in the very early pre-school years.[2]

2. Admission of both boys and girls. Recognizing from the start the preponderance of boys over girls among psychotic children, we provided twice as many beds for boys as for girls.

---

[2] In an effort to test the availability of pre-school children, we opened our intake for one year to children below five years of age; and we noted a more consistent tendency for these pre-school children to show clear-cut autistic features, together with more manifest neurological impairments and considerably lower intellectual and communicative competence.

3. Admission of children of all races, creeds, colors and socio-economic classes. However, the selective nature of this sample of psychotic children is emphasized. Factors other than arbitrary intake decision account for such selective sampling. They reflect the history of social service organizations in New York City, the influences of sectarian support and administration and the shifting nature of class and racial utilization of therapuetic resources. For example, our earliest analysis of the social class composition of our children showed an unusually high number of upper class families (Goldfarb, 1961), very much in accord with other studies of early childhood psychosis. In recent years, however, there has been a shift to children from poor families — in all likelihood, a reflection of the burgeoning number of social agencies concerned with the problems of the poor.

4. Admission of children from structurally intact homes. This criterion was adopted in order to be able to observe the role of the psychotic child in the intact family with all family members living together. (More recently we have been admitting psychotic children from fragmented families to observe the part played by family disruption. These children, however, have not been included in the present study). Of the 78 children in the study, all but one have come from structurally intact homes with father and mother living together.

5. Absence of known and manifest localizing signs of sensory and motor dysfunction and epilepsy. The primary symptoms are psychiatric. While we have always been aware of the unusual extent of neurological dysfunction and mental retardation in our psychotic children, these impairments have been delineated even after children with primary and unequivocal neurological impairments and primary mental retardation have been screened out and sent to appropriate social and medical services which specialize primarily in the study and care of such childhood disorders.

The Children

A total of 78 psychotic children treated in residence at the Ittleson Center and their families have been followed by the research psychiatrist. Age data are presented in Table 1. The children had entered treatment at a mean age of 7.2 years and had been discharged four years

Table 1

Age data of children in follow-up

Mean age at admission	7.2 years
Mean age at discharge	11.2 years
Mean age at last follow-up	19.9 years
Mean duration follow-up	8.7 years
Mean duration of total observation	12.7 years
(residential treatment plus follow-up)	

later at 11.2 years of age. Following discharge from the residence, they had been followed for 8.7 years, so that the mean age of the group at last follow-up was 19.9 years. At last follow-up, the subjects ranged in age between 13 years and 8 months and 29 years. Among the subjects, 52.6% were below 19 years of age and 47.4% were 19 years or older (Table 2). The total period of observation, embodying both periods of residential treatment and of subsequent follow-up, averaged 12.7 years. There is a range of individual difference in age of last follow-up and in duration of follow-up after discharge from the residence. The ultimate completion of assays of adult outcome in all the children will be possible when all the children reach adulthood.

Table 2

Age distribution at last follow-up

Age		Number	Per Cent
Less than 15	years	4	5.1
15—18.9	years	37	47.5
19—22.9	years	22	28.2
23 +	years	15	19.2
	Total	78	100.0

As described in Table 3, the great bulk of the children were white (89.7%) and the remainder were black and Hispanic. Approximately three-quarters of the children were Jewish in religious background. The remainder were distributed among Catholic, Protestant and other religions.

Table 4 summarizes the social and economic position of the families of the children, as classified with the Hollingshead-Redlich Index of Social Position. The families included a somewhat higher proportion of

Table 3

Race and religion of children

			Number	Per cent
A.	Race:	White	70	89.7
		Black	6	7.7
		Hispanic	2	2.6
		Total	78	100.0
B.	Religion:	Jewish	58	74.4
		Catholic	15	19.2
		Protestant	3	3.8
		Other	2	2.6
		Total	78	100.0

Table 4

Socio-economic position (Hollingshead-Redlich Index of Social Position) of families

Class description		Per cent of families	
		Psychotic	Normal*
1.	Upper	5.1	2.7
2.	Upper Middle	15.4	9.8
3.	Middle	25.7	18.9
4.	Low Middle	34.6	48.4
5.	Lower	19.2	20.2
	Total	100.0	100.0

* Hollingshead-Redlich population

middle to upper class families than the standardization population of Hollingshead and Redlich (1958). The data would thus seem to support the observations of numerous reporters, beginning with Kanner, (Kanner, 1954; Lotter, 1974; Rimland, 1965; and Rutter & Lockyer, 1967) that the families of young psychotic children cluster at upper socio-economic class levels. However, our own data are only suggestive in this regard; and in any case, a sizeable proportion of the families at the Ittleson Center are at lower class levels. We have also noted the increasing influx of poor families during the past ten years.

The population followed in the present study included 59 boys and 19 girls (Table 5). The ratio of boys to girls was 3.1 to 1. This proportion was close to that noted in previous Ittleson Center studies (Meyers & Goldfarb, 1962). Similarly, it confirmed the general trends in data of all

Table 5

Neurological Status	Sex and neurological status					
	Male		Female		Total	
	Number	Per cent	Number	Per cent	Number	Per cent
Organic	41	69.5	9	47.4	50	64.1
Non-organic	18	30.5	10	52.6	28	35.9
Total	59	100.0	19	100.0	78	100.0

observers of childhood psychosis who uniformly describe the higher proportion of boys over girls.

Diagnostic study of the children admitted to Ittleson Center includes independent neurological appraisal by a pediatric neurologist who takes a neurological history and examines the child neurologically. As reported above, in our intake studies, we have referred children with unequivocal localizing signs, abnormal reflexes and manifest sensory and motor impairments to neurological services at other institutions and hospitals. In a psychiatric installation such as the Ittleson Center, therefore, the neurological appraisal tends to rely more on patterned behavior of developmental significance. It emphasizes motor coordination and overflow, balance, gait, posture, muscle tone, perception, cognition, communication, and such global qualities as concentration, attention and activity level. On this basis and despite the exclusion of children with unequivocal evidence of neurological impairment, 64.1% of the children manifested neurological dysfunction, while 35.9% were regarded as free of neurological dysfunction (Table 5). The distribution of boys and girls by organicity is also presented.

The range of adaptive or integrative capacity of the children on admission to residential treatment may be demonstrated by employing the appraisals of ego status by the psychiatrists. The Ego Status Scale used by the psychiatrists is a five step scale which emphasizes observable manifestations of adaptive capacity and incorporates all the information available from the psychotherapy of the child as well as the extensive data provided by educational, child caring, psychological and social work staffs. The definitions of each step in the scale are appropriate for early school age children and have emerged out of direct experience with these children. They also reflect the working proposition that childhood psychosis represents developmental deficits in many aspects of ego organization, especially relational behavior, perception and cognition, social maturity, self care and educational response.

Figure 1 defines each of the five steps on the Ego Status Scale. At each step a global or summed judgment is based on observations of the

Figure 1. Scale for psychiatric appraisal of ego status in early school age

Level of Impairment	Definition	Rating
Very severely impaired	No differentiation of important persons, e.g. mother, from others; makes no contact with anybody; no speech or gestural communication, total or near-total avoidance of looking and listening; indiscriminate mouthing and smelling; near total absence of self care; no educability.	1
Severely impaired	Human preferences observable but misidentifications of important persons occur often; limited contact; speech and gestural communication below level of three year old (echoic, pronouns confused; comprehensibility below 90 per cent); mouthing and smelling still prominent, self care below that of a three year old; minimal educability (at pre-school level).	2
Moderately impaired	Recognition of and responses to important persons, contacting behavior (approaching, talking to others); speech and gestural communication above that of a three year old; responds to school education above grade 1; yet gross distortions of reality (body image, capacities, etc.) and psychotic behavior.	3
Mildly impaired	Mild eccentricity and no friends but functions acceptably in relation to school (including community school and with or without special adjustment such as ungraded class or special tutoring) and in relation to the external environment; or no longer manifestly outlandish or bizarre in relationship to people, school and the external environment but neurotic defenses present (e.g. obsessional or phobic).	4
Normal	By ordinary observation, child functioning well socially and educationally.	5

child's differentiation of important persons in his life, his mode of contacting others, his communication and speech, his receptor behavior, his level of self care and his educational response. Obviously, the five step intervals are not equal; but they are easily distinguished from each other, they do represent ranked status and ratings which have been shown to be very reliable (Goldfarb, Goldfarb & Pollack, 1966). As noted in Table 6, on admission, when the children were all manifesting active, patent psychotic reaction, they all fell between levels 1 and 3 on the Ego Status Scale. While all were psychotic, they were nevertheless highly diversified. For example, the children ranged from those devoid of apparent fantasy and totally lacking in language and capacity to care for themselves to children who were highly verbal in their discourse, embroiled in active, rich fantasy and, at times overideational.

Table 6

Ego status on admission to residential treatment

Ego status on admission	Number	Per cent
1. Very severely impaired	13	16.7
2. Severely impaired	37	47.4
3. Moderately impaired	28	35.9
4. Mildly impaired	0	0.0
5. Normal	0	0.0
Total	78	100.0

The children's ratings in intelligence tests may also be used to delineate the range of adaptive capacity at admission. Table 7 shows the distribution of full IQs in the Wechsler Intelligence Scale for Children. A majority of the children had IQs below 90 and 15.4% were so low in capacity as to be unscorable in the test. However, the children ranged from markedly retarded to superior levels of capacity.

Table 7

Distribution of Wechsler Intelligence Scale for Children on admission to residential treatment

WISC Full IQ on admission	Number	Per cent
Below 46	12	15.4
46—69	16	20.5
70—89	25	32.1
90—109	16	20.5
110 and above	9	11.5
Total	78	100.0

Appraisals of change and social outcomes

As in a previous analysis (Goldfarb, 1970) of follow-up changes in children discharged during the first ten years of operation of the residential program at the Ittleson Center, we have found it practi-

cable and profitable to employ the following sources of information for the assay of change in clinical and social status:
1. psychiatric appraisals of ego status.
2. life course of the children, expressed in their placement at home, in the community, or in a specialized institution.

To appraise changes in ego status in the course of their treatment at the Ittleson Center, we have utilized psychiatric appraisals of ego status, based on the definitions of the above described Ego Status Scale. These psychiatric appraisals enable the observer to record developmental improvement and to note the child's ability to cope with the ordinary expectancies of family and community life with normal degree of independence and self reliance. Our longitudinal investigations (Goldfarb, 1970, 1974) have already demonstrated the strong trend to measurable ego improvement in the majority of psychotic children while in residential treatment, particularly if one excludes the most drastically impaired, cerebrally restricted children from consideration. However, these studies have also demonstrated that only a small portion of the children achieved normal levels of behavioral response. Since we were already certain that some degree of adaptive improvement might be expected in a large portion of psychotic children with language and measurable capacity, in this study we were additionally interested in the rates and patterns of normalization. At each point of observation, we asked if the child had reached near normal (that is, mildly impaired) to normal levels of functional organization.

Placement of the psychotic child with his family, rather than in an institution specializing in the care of the exceptional child, is a coarse criterion of adaptive improvement in the child. Such placement is determined in large measure by parental capacity and motivation to care for the child as well as by the child's clinical status. Nevertheless, the coping capacity of the child undoubtedly plays a role in the family decision to place the child or to keep him at home. In addition, the central construct in our therapeutic intervention has been the active enhancement of the family's role in strengthening and supporting the forward progress of each child's ego organization. It must be noted that the initial placement of these children in the residence was a last step decision after other treatment plans had been attempted and when it was felt that separation from the family would be therapeutic and profitable for the child. On this basis, we regard the life course of the child, expressed in placement history, as a valid as well as practical criterion of social outcome. That is to say, if the child was able to go home, we regarded this as evidence of growth and improvement in the relational systems of the child with his family and with the community.

To appraise psychiatric outcome in follow-up when the children were in their teens or older we employed a modification of the Ego Status Scale (See Figure 2). This modification paralleled the scale developed for use during residential treatment when the children were younger and permitted comparisons of the children at admission to the residence, at discharge from the residence and at later follow-up. While referring to developmental considerations pertinent for each age, we have continued to use the five ratings of ego status at each point of observation. As in the original descriptions of the Ego Status Scale, ratings 1 to 3 (moderate to very severe impairment) represent grossly impaired functioning of children with manifest psychotic behavior and ego disabilities of such serious degree and quality as to warrant residential treatment or a comparable form of comprehensive treatment. Ratings 4 and 5 (mild impairment and normal) characterize functioning of children capable of coping with the

Figure 2. Scale for psychiatric appraisal of ego status in adolescence

Level of Impairment	Definition	Rating
Very severely impaired	Total impairment in purposeful functions, so that capacity for self care, communication, relationship and orientation is totally lacking.	1
Severely impaired	Severe, but not total, impairment in purposeful functions. Capacity for self care, communication, relationship and orientation very deficient.	2
Moderately impaired	Behavior grossly disturbed and capacity for independent existence meagre; but superior to 2 and there is a measure of social capacity and responsiveness.	3
Mildly impaired	Mild eccentricity and few friends, but functions acceptably in relation to school, including a community school and with or without special adjustment such as ungraded class, and in relation to external environment; or no longer manifestly outlandish or bizarre in relationship to people, school and external environment but neurotic defenses are present.	4
Normal	By ordinary observation, child functioning well socially and educationally.	5

requirements of life in the family and community, even though they may still be showing areas of deviancy in personality.

As we have previously noted (Goldfarb, 1970), the Ittleson Center definitions of ego status in follow-up approximate the definitions of other observers of adolescent adjustment of psychotic children (Eisenberg, 1956; Rutter, 1965). This overlap in definitions supports the pertinence and validity of the categories used in the present study.

Eisenberg's definitions of social adjustment in adolescence are as follows:

"*Good*: patient functioning well academically and socially; *Fair*: patient able to attend school at about grade level but distinctly deviant in personality; *Poor*: patient shows maladaptive functioning, characterized by apparent feeble-mindedness and/or grossly disturbed psychotic behavior."

Rutter's definitions of social adjustment used by other observers such as Lotter (1974) are as follows:

Good: child having normal social life and functioning satisfactorily at school or at work; *Fair*: child making social and educational progress in spite of significant, even marked abnormalities in behavior or interpersonal relationships; *Poor*: child severely handicapped and unable to lead an independent life, but where there is still some measure of social adjustment and some remaining potential for social adjustment; *Very poor*: child unable to lead any kind of independent existence."

A figure relating ratings used in the Ittleson follow-up studies to those by Eisenberg and Rutter is presented in Figure 3. The Ittleson Center "normal" rating coincides with the "good" ratings of both

Figure 3. Ratings* of outcome in follow-up studies of psychotic children

Ittleson Center	Eisenberg	Rutter
Grossly impaired ego	Poor	—
Very severe impairment	—	Very poor
Moderate to severe impairment	—	Poor
Mildly impaired to normal ego		
Mild impairment	Fair	Fair
Normal	Good	Good

*Ratings on a horizontal line are equivalent in definition.

Eisenberg and Rutter; and the "mild impairment" rating at Ittleson Center compares more roughly with the "fair" ratings of Eisenberg and Rutter. Our "grossly impaired" ego categories are paralleled by Eisenberg's "poor" and Rutter's "very poor" and "poor" categories of adjustment.

Statistical treatment

In this report, the probabilities used in connection with levels of significance have been selected to be more stringent tests of relationships than applied in an earlier follow-up study based on the Fisher Exact Probability and Chi square tests (Goldfarb, 1970). Thus, we use probabilities of .05 or less as a basis for rejecting the null hypothesis. Two tailed tests of rejection have generally also been employed in the present study, even where it has been feasible to predict the direction of relationships. In some of the Tables, it was necessary to combine cell frequencies in order to conduct a chi square test. (Even then, the cell frequencies were sometimes small but we still thought it useful to retain the chi square tests.) In what follows, it may be presumed, therefore, that all references to significant findings meet these statistical tests of significance. A summary of findings which are statistically significant $(p < .05)$ in the tables which follow is presented in Figure 4. To force the columns of percentages to add up to 100.0, the largest included percentage was accordingly changed in the decimal position.

Longitudinal patterns of change

In the analysis to follow, we shall first appraise each child in terms of his characteristic profile of longitudinal change during the period between his admission to treatment and his discharge from treatment (average 4.0 years) and then between his discharge from treatment and last follow-up (average 8.7 years).

Our appraisals of ego status of the children at each of the three points in time—that is, admission, discharge, follow-up—permit us to categorize each child in terms of individual patterns of change. Such individual profiles of longitudinal change may be accomplished as follows:

(1) Establish the criterion of normalcy which we define as a rating of either mild impairment (ego level 4) or normal (ego level 5) in the Ego Status Scale. (Although more gross, an alternative criterion of normalcy is placement at home in the community.)

(2) Classify whether the criterion is not met (ego levels 1 - 3) and code this condition 0; or whether the criterion is met (ego levels 4 - 5) and code this as condition 1.

(3) Record this two-way classification at admission, discharge and follow-up. On this basis, eight curves of change are theoretically possible as follows:

Figure 4. A summary of findings which are statistically significant (p $<$ .05)

Tables		Significant	Not significant
5			X
9	Admission to discharge	X	
	discharge to follow-up	X	
12		X	
14			X
15			X
16		X	
17			X
18			X
19			X
20			X
21			X
22			X
23			X
24			X
25			X
26			X
27			X
28			X
29	Social classes 1, 2, 3 combined	X	
30	Ego status 2, 3 combined*	X	
31	Ego status 2, 3 combined*	X	
32	IQ $<$ vs. 46 & above*	X	
33	*	X	
34	IQ $<$ vs. 46 & above	X	
35	*	X	
36	Ego status 1, 2 combined	X	
37	Ego status 1, 2 combined	X	
38	Combined IQ below 70 & combined IQ 90 & above	X	
39	Combined IQ below 70 & combined IQ 90 & above	X	
40	Ego status 2, 3 combined	X	
	Ego status 1, 2 combined	X	
41	Ego status 2, 3 combined	X	
	Ego status 1, 2 combined		
42	Combined IQ below 70 & combined IQ 90 & above	X	
43	Combined IQ below 70 & combined IQ 90 & above	X	
44	Ego status 1, 2 combined and 3, 4 combined	X	
45	Ego status 1, 2, 3 combined	X	
46			X
47			X
48			X
49			X

Figure 4. (continued)

Tables	Significant	Not significant
50		X
51		X
52		X
53		X
54		X
55		X
56		X
57	X	
58	X	
59	X	
60		X
61		X

*However small frequencies noted.

*Code 0   means that child does not meet the criterion of normalcy at
           the stated point in time.

Code 1   means that the child does meet the criterion of normalcy at
           the stated point in time.

Example: Code B, 0-0-1, indicates the child did not meet the criterion of normalcy until
           the last follow-up.

(4) Since all the children did not meet the criterion of normalcy at admission and are, therefore, coded (0) for ego status at admission to treatment, only the four patterns of change in ego status in the left section (A, B, C, D) are, in fact, possible.

We are primarily interested in these total longitudinal patterns of the individual children, as they change between admission and last follow-up. But the total incidence of children who meet the criterion of normalcy at each of the three points is also of interest, that is admission, discharge and last follow up, and is easily determined by summating the data for the appropriate curves. Thus, none of the children met the criterion of normalcy at admission. The total number of children who met the criterion at discharge is obtained by adding the children who showed curves C and D and the number of children who met the criterion at follow-up is obtained by adding children who showed curves B and D.

In the analysis of changes in ego status to follow, therefore, after summarizing the distribution of individual curves, we shall summarize group data separately at the time the children were admitted to treatment, at time of discharge from treatment and at the time of later follow-up, to test whether significant changes for the total group occur with the passage of time in ego status (and in placement).

In Table 8, it is shown that 24.4% of the children, a significant proportion, attained mildly impaired to normal levels of ego integration by discharge from treatment and continued to meet the criterion of normalcy at last follow-up (Pattern D). An equal and significant proportion did not achieve the criterion of normalcy at discharge; but then improved sufficiently in ego after discharge so that they met the criterion at last follow-up (Pattern B). Almost four percent of the children attained the criterion of normalcy by discharge from treatment but declined in ego status after leaving the residential treatment center (Pattern C). (As will be seen, all the children who declined in follow-up were further classified as non-organic and male.)

Table 8

Patterns of change in ego status with regard to the criterion of normalcy
(ego status 4 and 5)

Criterion Pattern		Number	Per cent
A	0-0-0	37	47.4
B	0-0-1	19	24.4
C	0-1-0	3	3.8
D	0-1-1	19	24.4
	Total	78	100.0

Summarizing the same data at each of the three points of observation (Table 9), it is apparent that in contrast to their status at admission, 28.2% of the children demonstrated mildly impaired to normal levels of ego at discharge from treatment and 48.7% of the children at last follow-up attained such near-normal levels of social and psychiatric outcome. The group improvement to these levels of ego during residential treatment was statistically significant (p.$<$.01). However, it is striking that a significant number of additional children attained mildly impaired to normal levels of ego status (Ego level 4 and 5) during the period of follow-

Table 9

Ego status at admission to residential treatment,
discharge and last follow-up

Ego status	Admission		Discharge		Follow-up	
	Number	Per cent	Number	Per cent	Number	Per cent
Mildly impaired to normal*	0	0.0	22	28.2	38	48.7
Grossly impaired **	78	100.0	56	71.8	40	51.3
Total	78	100.0	78	100.0	78	100.0

* Levels 4, 5 ** Levels 1, 2, 3

up after discharge from residential treatment (p.<.01). It should be noted also that while 28.2% of the children met the criterion of normalcy at discharge, all of these children were rated ego level 4 (mildly impaired) and there were no children rated ego level 5 (normal) at this time. In contrast, at follow-up, nine children (11.5%) attained normal ego ratings (ego level 5).

We may also consider individual patterns of change with regard to life course (Table 10). Here our criterion of normalcy is placement at home and in the community. Failure to meet the criterion is represented in placement in a specialized institution for the psychotic or developmentally retarded child. Since all the children were psychotic and placed in a residential treatment center on admission to treatment, only four patterns of individual change are again possible.

Table 10

Patterns of change in placement with regard to the criterion of
normalcy (home placement)

Criterion Pattern		Number	Per cent
A	0-0-0	10	12.8
B	0-0-1	8	10.3
C	0-1-0	12	15.4
D	0-1-1	48	61.5
	Total	78	100.0

Ten of the children (12.8%) remained in institutional care throughout the entire period of observation (Pattern A). The greatest proportion (61.5%) of the children were discharged home after residential treatment and were still at home in the community at follow-up (Pattern D). A significant percentage (15.4%) were sent home after residential treatment but had been returned subsequently to institutions at time of last follow-up (Pattern C). However 10.3% were continued in institutions after discharge but were later returned home (Pattern B).

Table 11 presents the number and percent of children who met the criterion of normalcy with regard to placement at discharge from residential treatment and at last follow-up. Now it can be seen that a considerably higher percent were able ultimately to live in the community than attained mildly impaired to normal levels of ego status (See Table 9). Thus 76.9% of the children were returned to their families at discharge from residential treatment and 71.8% were living with their families at last follow-up, whereas only 28.2% and 48.7% attained mildly impaired to normal levels of ego status. Those children who could not be cared for at home were found in mental hospitals, institutions for the retarded and other varieties of group care for emotionally disturbed children.

Table 11

Placement at discharge from residential treatment, and
at last follow-up

Placement	Discharge		Follow-up	
	Number	Per cent	Number	Per cent
Home	60	76.9	56	71.8
Institution	18	23.1	22	28.2
Total	78	100.0	78	100.0

We have previously called attention to the apparent disparity between the large percentage of the children who returned home at discharge or those at home in follow-up and the smaller proportion of children who attained only mildly impaired to normal levels of ego organization (Ego levels 4, 5). This indicates that some children with continuing evidence of serious personality deviations have been able to return to their families and to live within the community.

The relationship for the child between ego status and the life arrangement at last follow-up is shown in Table 12. All but three of the 38 children (92.1%) with mildly impaired to normal ego status (Ego levels 4 and 5) were to be found in their homes and in the community. The three children with such mildly impaired to normal levels of ego organization who nevertheless were to be found in institutions included two well-

Table 12

Ego status and placement at last follow-up

Placement		Ego Status		
		Grossly impaired		Mildly impaired to normal
		Number	Per cent	Number	Per cent
Home		21	52.5	35	92.1
Institution		19	47.5	3	7.9
Total		40	100.0	38	100.0

adjusted mental retardates from normal families who were living in a specialized educational environment for such retardates. The third child required a group placement in spite of normal social and emotional adjustment, because of a broken home which was unable to care for him. One may conclude that the children who attained ego status levels 4 and 5 at follow-up were all living with their families in the community, provided these families were functionally intact and provided the children did not need the specialized education and training required by the cerebrally impaired mental retardate.

The relationship between ego status and placement is less precise than just noted in the case of children with grossly impaired levels of ego status (Ego levels 1 - 3) at last follow-up. While grossly impaired in ego, more than half (52.5%) were living at home.

As reported in the previous follow-up study of the children treated at the Ittleson Center and discharged within the first ten years of its operation (Goldfarb, 1970), parents were often impelled to bring even grossly impaired children back home after discharge as the children entered adolescence. While these children were still presenting evidences of psychosis at that time, many of the parents had been helped to achieve greater confidence and skill in the care and management of the children. In this regard the parents had been able to observe the responsiveness and manageability of the children within the rather calm, unafraid and child invested atmosphere of the residence. In addition, while not attaining normal ego levels, many of these grossly impaired children had, in fact, demonstrated a perceptible degree of improvement in adaptive and social response. Apart from whether they achieved the criterion of normalcy, in agreement with previous studies (Goldfarb, 1970, 1974), the children demonstrated clear growth and improvement in social and adaptive competence during residential treatment (Table 13). Indeed, 60.3% of the children showed improvement, as expressed in a rise of at least one step interval in the Ego Status Scale (p. $<$.01) and no child declined in status during residential treatment. Within this framework,

Table 13

Psychiatric rating of ego status at admission to residential treatment and discharge; by number of children

Ego Status at Admission	Ego Status at Discharge					
	1	2	3	4	5	Total
1	7	3	3	0	0	13
2	0	10	19	8	0	37
3	0	0	14	14	0	28
Total	7	13	36	22	0	78

the professional staff tended to support the children in their desire to return home, particularly when this represented a hopeful craving for more permanent and enduring human relationships than were available in the residence. The clinical staff was also inclined to identify with the parents when they expressed an uncomplicated and wholesome desire to take care of the children and to take responsibility for the children as they moved through their adolescence. It should be understood, too, that from an empirical point of view we had been able to confirm that many of our children, particularly in the organic universe of psychotic children, could be treated as effectively in day treatment as in residential treatment, provided that the families were intact and that a flexible, educational, socially rehabilitative, and therapeutic program of support was offered to them.

Factors associated with outcome

For the first time in our longitudinal investigations, we are in a position to appraise the links between the clinical and integrative status of the child suffering from early childhood psychosis during his early years and his status in adolescence and early adult years. In the present analysis, interest centers primarily on the association between a number of independent factors and the child's status at last follow-up when the mean age of the children was 19.9 years. We have, of course, been conscious of the uniqueness and homogeneous character of the social environment of the residential treatment center and its differences from the diverse environments provided the children when they were returned to their families at discharge. Because we do not know the comparative effects of these environments, we have separated longitudinal changes in the children during residential treatment (admission to discharge) from changes noted in follow-up after residential treatment (discharge to last follow-up). In the discussion to follow, too, we shall be noting changes in the status of the children at three points in time, namely, admission to residential treatment, discharge from treatment and last follow-up.

Outcomes at last follow-up are of particular interest since they are most closely linked in time to the ultimate life course of psychotic children. For evaluating parameters linked with outcome at follow-up, we shall consider the same factors studied in relation to time of discharge. In addition, it will now be possible to evaluate the predictive significance of the ego status of the children on discharge from residential treatment. Again we shall be defining social and psychiatric outcomes in terms of two large levels of adjustment. One level refers to grossly impaired functioning (Ego Status 1, 2, 3). The other refers to mild impairment or normal adjustment (Ego Status 4, 5) — a level where the child is able to cope with the ordinary stresses of community and school (or job) with an average degree of autonomy and self reliance. As noted in our previous discussions, the latter constitutes our criterion of normalcy.

The design of the follow-up study permits the evaluation of association between social and psychiatric outcomes at last follow-up and the following factors: neurological integrity of the child, socio-economic position of the family, ego status at admission to residential treatment, ego status at discharge from residential treatment, sex of the child and age of admission to treatment. Specific features of therapeutic intake, sample selection and mode of treatment, have precluded the consideration of several other factors. Thus, at admission, all the children but one (98.7%) came from structurally intact homes with father and mother living together, so that the part played by overt structural breakups in the families cannot be considered. Amount of schooling as a factor cannot be evaluated, since the therapeutic design required all the children to attend school throughout the period of residential treatment.

Neurological Integrity

Neurological status of the child will first be considered inasmuch as a number of studies have demonstrated that psychotic children with evident neurological dysfunction (whom we shall call "organic" children) differ in many ways from psychotic children free of evidence of neurological dysfunction (whom we shall call "non-organic" children). These two subsets of psychotic children, distinguished by neurological appraisal of history and physical examination, are different in sex distribution since the organic children have a higher proportion of boys than the non-organic children (Goldfarb, 1961, 1970, 1974; Meyers

& Goldfarb, 1962). They differ in abilities, inasmuch as non-organic children are superior in a broad range of cognitive, motor and communicative abilities (Goldfarb, 1961, 1974). They differ in the functional levels of their families, in that organic children come from a broader range of families and more frequently have been reared in average families (Goldfarb, 1961). The patterns of longitudinal change have differed. For example, during treatment non-organic children have shown greater attainment than organic children (Goldfarb & Pollack, 1964). Finally, non-organic children have shown more growth in ego status while in residential treatment, even when non-organic and organic children have been matched in sex, IQ, and ego status at admission to treatment (Goldfarb, 1970).

When classified in this study with reference to the criterion of normalcy (Ego Status 4 or 5), differences between organic and non-organic children in patterns of change between admission and last follow-up are just above the selected level of significance (.05) and are, therefore, regarded as not statistically significant (Table 14). When

Table 14

Patterns of change in ego status with regard to the criterion of normalcy
(ego status 4 and 5): organic and non-organic children

Criterion Pattern		Organic		Non-Organic	
		Number	Per cent	Number	Per cent
A	0-0-0	27	54.0	10	35.8
B	0-0-1	13	26.0	6	21.4
C	0-1-0	0	0.0	3	10.7
D	0-1-1	10	20.0	9	32.1
	Total	50	100.0	28	100.0

placement at home is employed as the criterion of normalcy, the organic and non-organic subsets are again not found to be significantly different in profiles of change (Table 15).

As in the prior study (Goldfarb, 1970), the present study confirms that during the period of residential treatment, a significantly greater proportion of non-organic children showed improvement in ego status than organic children. At discharge, a higher proportion of non-organic children than organic children attained near normal to normal levels of ego organization (Table 16). Proportionately speaking, about twice as many non-organic children reached near normal levels of ego or better at this time.

Table 15

Patterns of change in placement with regard to criterion of normalcy (home placement): organic and non-organic children

Criterion Pattern		Organic		Non-Organic	
		Number	Per cent	Number	Per cent
A	0-0-0	9	18.0	2	7.1
B	0-0-1	4	8.0	4	14.3
C	0-1-0	8	16.0	4	14.3
D	0-1-1	29	58.0	18	64.3
	Total	50	100.0	28	100.0

Table 16

Ego status at discharge from residential treatment: organic and non organic children

Ego Status at Discharge	Organic		Non-Organic	
	Number	Per cent	Number	Per cent
Mildly impaired to normal	10	20.0	12	42.9
Grossly impaired	40	80.0	16	57.1
Total	50	100.0	28	100.0

While the non-organic children showed more improvement in ego status than organic children by time of discharge, and despite the repeated evidence of intrinsically greater all around adaptive competence of non-organic children than organic children, the two subsets of psychotic children did not differ significantly in proportion of children discharged to their homes on completion of residential treatment (Table 17). In both groups of children, a majority of the children returned to their homes and were living in the community. As in the earlier study

Table 17

Placement at discharge from residential treatment: organic and non-organic children

Placement at Discharge	Organic		Non-Organic	
	Number	Per cent	Number	Per cent
Home	37	74.0	22	78.6
Institution	13	26.0	6	21.4
Total	50	100.0	28	100.0

(Goldfarb, 1970), therefore, we are impressed with the fact that the two groups did not differ in placement at discharge, even though a greater proportion of non-organic children had attained higher ego levels and greater general capacity to meet the expectable challenges of ordinary family and community living. We have surmised a number of contributing factors. For example, we have observed a powerful disposition on the part of some families of organic children to reabsorb the children despite conspicuous incapacities in the children. On the other hand, after comprehensive treatment, we have also noted in these children an adequate capacity to respond and accommodate to the emotional and social requirements of family life despite gross incapacities in other areas of purposeful response.

Table 18 summarizes findings at last follow-up for children with evidence of neurological dysfunction (organic children), as diagnosed at the beginning of residential treatment, and children free of such evidence of neurological dysfunction (non-organic children). The two subsets of psychotic children, classified by neurological appraisal of history and physical examination, showed no significant difference in ego status at last follow-up. Similarly, as noted in Table 19, the two subclusters of children did not differ significantly at that time in percent of individuals living at home rather than in a specialized institution for the emotionally disturbed.

Table 18

Ego status at last follow-up: organic and non-organic children

Ego Status at Last Follow-up	Organic		Non-Organic	
	Number	Per cent	Number	Per cent
Mildly impaired to normal	23	46.0	15	53.6
Grossly impaired	27	54.0	13	46.4
Total	50	100.0	28	100.0

Table 19

Placement at last follow up: organic and non-organic children

Placement at last Follow-up	Organic		Non-organic	
	Number	Per cent	Number	Per cent
Home	33	66.0	22	78.6
Institution	17	34.0	6	21.4
Total	50	100.0	28	100.0

Again, as in our previous follow-up investigation (Goldfarb, 1970), non-organic children showed a significantly superior response to residential treatment in that a higher percentage of non-organic than organic children had reached the criterion of normalcy of ego organization (Ego Status 4, 5) by discharge. However, in the 8.7 years following discharge from treatment, this difference between the two subsets of psychotic children was not sustained. While both subgroups showed improvements in ego status in follow-up, so as to move from grossly impaired levels to near normal or even normal levels of ego organization, we may infer that the organic children were more inclined to maintain such improvement. As noted in Table 8, examination of the profiles of individual children during follow-up demonstrated that three of the children, who had reached slightly impaired to normal levels (Ego Status 4, 5) by the end of residential treatment, had decompensated and declined to grossly impaired, manifestly psychotic levels at the time of last follow-up. All these instances of decompensation were boys in the non-organic subcluster. (This finding parallels those of the earlier study in 1970.) Thus, the more consistent trend among organic children toward sustaining growth in ego in the period following discharge from residential treatment offset the more successful response of the non-organic children to residential treatment.

As we have noted, neurological status of psychotic children is associated with sex and ego status of the children. To eliminate the possible confounding effects of sex and ego status at start of treatment, 24 organic children were matched with 24 non-organic children in sex and ego status at admission. A comparison of these two groups offers support for previously noted findings for the entire group (Tables 20 - 23). While proportionately more non-organic than organic children attained mildly impaired to normal levels in residential treatment, the differences are now not statistically significant. Again, in follow-up 7.9 years after discharge, there were no significant differences in ego status.

Table 20

Ego status at discharge of organic children and non-organic children, matched in sex and in ego status at admission

Ego Status at Discharge	Organic		Non-organic	
	Number	Per cent	Number	Per cent
Mildly impaired to normal	5	20.8	10	41.7
Grossly impaired	19	79.2	14	58.3
Total	24	100.0	24	100.0

Table 21

Placement at discharge of organic children and non-organic children, matched in sex and in ego status at admission

Ego Status at Discharge	Organic		Non-organic	
	Number	Per cent	Number	Per cent
Home	17	70.8	18	75.0
Institution	7	29.2	6	25.0
Total	24	100.0	24	100.0

Table 22

Ego status at last follow-up of organic children and non-organic children, matched in sex and in ego status at admission

Ego Status at last Follow-up	Organic		Non-organic	
	Number	Per cent	Number	Per cent
Mildly impaired to normal	13	54.2	12	50.0
Grossly impaired	11	45.8	12	50.0
Total	24	100.0	24	100.0

Table 23

Placement at last follow-up of organic children and non-organic children, matched in sex and ego status at admission

Placement at last Follow-up	Organic		Non-organic	
	Number	Per cent	Number	Per cent
Home	13	54.2	18	75.0
Institution	11	45.8	6	25.0
Total	24	100.0	24	100.0

In addition, the two groups did not differ in percent of children placed at home at discharge from treatment and in percent living at home at last follow-up. These carefully matched cases, therefore, support the inference of no differences between organic and non-organic subsets of psychotic children at time of last follow-up.

Socio-economic position[4]

In previous reports, we have stressed significant differences in adaptive competence among psychotic children derived from

---

[4]Hollingshead-Redlich Index of Social Position (Hollingshead & Redlich, 1958).

families of different socio-economic status. Thus, there has been an inverse relationship between intellectual functioning (IQ) of the psychotic child and socio-economic position of the family, with children of lowest socio-economic position highest in mean IQ, children from families of highest socio-economic position lowest in mean IQ, and children of families at middle socio-economic position intermediate in mean IQ (Goldfarb, 1974). It is, therefore, of interest that the children of different social classes, as measured with the Hollingshead-Redlich Index of Social Position, did not differ in regard to the four profiles of change, employing our criteria of normalcy with regard to both ego status and placement course (Tables 24, 25).

Table 24

Patterns of change in ego status with regard to the criterion of normalcy
(ego status 4 and 5): socio-economic position
(Hollingshead-Redlich Index of Social Position)

| | | Socio-economic Position | | | | | |
| | | Upper (Class 1 & 2) | | Middle (Class 3) | | Lower (Class 4 & 5) | |
Criterion Pattern		Number	Per cent	Number	Per cent	Number	Per cent
A	0-0-0	6	40.0	11	55.0	20	46.5
B	0-0-1	3	20.0	6	30.0	10	23.3
C	0-1-0	2	13.3	0	0.0	1	2.3
D	0-1-1	4	26.7	3	15.0	12	27.9
	Total	15	100.0	20	100.0	43	100.0

Table 25

Patterns of change in placement with regard to the criterion
of normalcy (home placement): socio economic position
(Hollingshead-Redlich Index of Social Position)

| | | Socio-economic Position | | | | | |
| | | Upper (Class 1 & 2) | | Middle (Class 3) | | Lower (Class 4 & 5) | |
Criterion Pattern		Number	Per cent	Number	Per cent	Number	Per cent
A	0-0-0	4	26.7	3	15.0	4	9.3
B	0-0-1	1	6.7	2	10.0	5	11.6
C	0-1-0	4	26.7	4	20.0	4	9.3
D	0-1-1	6	40.0	11	55.0	30	69.8
	Total	15	100.1	20	100.0	43	100.0

At point of discharge, the children from families at varying socio-economic position did not differ from each other in ego status. Thus, as in Table 26, on ending residential treatment, there were no significant differences among the children when categorized by socio-economic position, so that children from poor families (Hollingshead-Redlich Index, classes 4, 5) did not differ significantly from children reared in middle to upper class families (Hollingshead-Redlich Scale Index, Classes 1, 2, 3) in percentage of children who attained mildly impaired to normal levels of ego status. Nor was socio-economic position significantly associated with the placement at discharge (Table 27).

Table 26

Ego status at discharge from residential treatment and socio-economic position
(Hollingshead-Redlich Index of Social Position)

Ego Status at Discharge	Socio-economic Position					
	Upper (Class 1 & 2)		Middle (Class 3)		Lower (Class 4 & 5)	
	Number	Per cent	Number	Per cent	Number	Per cent
Mildly impaired to Normal	6	40.0	3	15.0	13	30.2
Grossly impaired	9	60.0	17	85.0	30	69.8
Total	15	100.0	20	100.0	43	100.0

Table 27

Placement at discharge and socio-economic position
(Hollingshead-Redlich Index of Social Position)

Placement at Discharge	Socio-economic Position					
	Upper (Class 1 & 2)		Middle (Class 3)		Lower (Class 4 & 5)	
	Number	Per cent	Number	Per cent	Number	Per cent
Home	10	66.7	15	75.0	34	79.1
Institution	5	33.3	5	25.0	9	20.9
Total	15	100.0	20	100.0	43	100.0

As at discharge from treatment, socio-economic position of the families was not associated with ego status at last follow-up (Table 28). In other words, children from poor families were not distinguished from children in middle to upper class families in percent of children who attained mildly impaired to normal levels of ego status, the criterion of normalcy. However, these two subsets did differ in percentage located at

Table 28

Ego status at last follow-up and socio-economic position
(Hollingshead-Redlich Index of Social Position)

Ego Status at Discharge	Upper (Class 1 & 2)		Middle (Class 3)		Lower (Class 4 & 5)	
	Number	Per cent	Number	Per cent	Number	Per cent
Mildly impaired to normal	7	46.7	9	45.0	22	51.2
Grossly impaired	8	53.3	11	55.0	21	48.8
Total	15	100.0	20	100.0	43	100.0

home at this time (Table 29). More children from the poor families
(Hollingshead-Redlich Index, Classes 4, 5) were living at home or in the
community at follow-up. This may reflect the greater capacity of middle
to upper class families to pay for specialized institutional service. Or
conceivably, the poor families may be showing greater acceptance of the
children.

Table 29

Placement at last follow-up and socio-economic position
(Hollingshead-Redlich Index of Social Position)

Placement at last Follow-up	Socio-economic Position					
	Upper (Class 1 & 2)		Middle (Class 3)		Lower (Class 4 & 5)	
	Number	Per cent	Number	Per cent	Number	Per cent
Home	7	46.7	13	65.0	36	83.7
Institution	8	53.3	7	35.0	7	16.3
Total	15	100.0	20	100.0	43	100.0

Adaptive competence of child

As noted in our earlier discussion, in virtually all
follow-up investigations, including our own, the single dimension of
greatest power in predicting ultimate outcomes has been the adaptive
competence of the child in his early years. This conclusion is particularly
pertinent if one employs for predictive purposes the child's adaptive
status at five to seven years of age, a time when the child ordinarily
possesses a complex repertoire of capacities for self care, communication, active cognition, social responses and education enabling him to go
to school. Psychotic children characterized by the most extreme deficits
at this stage such as total lack of comprehensible language or of measur-

able intelligence in the well-known tests for early school age children, or children who, generally speaking, represent the most impaired of the broad range of psychotic children one encounters in a non-selective intake have shown in a highly predictable fashion very poor psychiatric and social outcomes in adolescence or later maturity.

As we have utilized it, the term ego status encompasses competence in a broad range of purposeful functions regulating the child's accommodation to his social and physical worlds. Thus, in our evaluation of ego status, we have preferred an evaluation which incorporates assays of the multiple aspects of ego which have been notably impaired in psychotic children, including the deficits in relational response, speech, receptor behavior, cognition, social maturity and response to education. We are, therefore, using as our primary datum the summed ratings of ego status made by psychiatrists, who based their judgments on all the very extensive information available in the course of comprehensive residential treatment and subsequent after care. However, we have demonstrated the high correlation between the ego status ratings by psychiatrists and other systematic measures of functional competence, such as performance in intelligence tests (Goldfarb, 1970). Since the latter are so universally employed and available, we shall also show the association between ultimate outcomes in follow-up and Full IQ in the Wechsler Intelligence Tests for Children at start of residential treatment at a mean age of 7.2 years.

Utilizing our criterion of normalcy in ego (ego status 4 or 5) children classified by ego at admission differed significantly among themselves in profiles of change (See Table 30). A majority of children rated in ego status at admission at levels of 1 and 2 did not ever attain normal status (criterion pattern A). Of the children rated ego status 1 at admission, all but one (92.3%) showed no improvement in treatment. But more than

Table 30

Patterns of change in ego status with regard to the criterion of normalcy
(ego status 4 and 5): ego status at admission

		Ego Status at Admission				
		Level 1		Level 2		Level 3	
Criterion Pattern		Number	Per cent	Number	Per cent	Number	Per cent
A	0-0-0	12	92.3	20	52.6	5	18.5
B	0-0-1	1	7.7	10	26.3	8	29.6
C	0-1-0	0	0.0	3	7.9	0	0.0
D	0-1-1	0	0.0	5	13.2	14	51.9
	Total	13	100.0	38	100.0	27	100.0

half of the children rated at admission at ego level 3 met the normal criterion at discharge and continued to do so at follow up (Pattern D) and almost another third met the criterion at latest follow-up (Pattern B).

The findings in regard to home placement as the criterion of normalcy also show significant differences based on ego status at admission, even though children at all levels of ego at admission were to be found at home at discharge and at follow-up (Table 31). The general trend toward association between ego status at admission and the normalcy criterion (home placement) is supported if, for example, one examines the portion of children at each ego level who show criterion pattern D (0-1-1).

Similar trends are found if the children are subdivided, utilizing WISC Full IQ as the measure of functional competence. Using ego status as the criterion of normalcy (ego status 4 and 5), children with IQs below 70 were significantly different from children with IQs 70 and above (Tables 32, 33). The children with IQs below 70 showed a higher proportion with the non-improving criterion pattern A (0-0-0) and a lower proportion with improvement patterns B and D (0-0-1 and 0-1-1). Again, utilizing home placement as our criterion of normalcy, children with IQs below 70 were clearly different from children with IQs 70 and above in regard to patterns of improvements (Tables 34, 35). Patterns of unchanging institutionalization (Pattern A) are particularly linked to lower IQ children. In contrast, criterion pattern D (0-1-1), denoting return to home on discharge and continued home placement through follow-up, was characteristic of the higher IQ subgroups.

Table 36 demonstrates the association between ego status at admission and ego status at discharge. It is apparent that, while all the children were psychotic at admission (ego levels 1, 2, and 3), the higher

Table 31

Patterns of change in placement with regard to the criterion of normalcy (home placement): ego status at admission

		Ego Status at Admission					
		Level 1		Level 2		Level 3	
Criterion Pattern		Number	Per cent	Number	Per cent	Number	Per cent
A	0-0-0	4	30.8	6	15.8	0	0.0
B	0-0-1	0	0.0	6	15.8	2	7.4
C	0-1-0	4	30.8	5	13.2	3	11.1
D	0-1-1	5	38.4	21	55.2	22	81.5
	Total	13	100.0	38	100.0	27	100.0

Table 32

Patterns of change in ego status with regard to the criterion of normalcy (ego status 4 and 5):
Wechsler Intelligence Scale for Children Full IQ at admission

	WISC Full IQ at Admission								
	Below 46		46–69		70–89		90–109		110 & above	
Criterion Pattern	Number	Per cent	Number	Per cent	Number	Per cent	Number	Per cent	Number	Per cent
A 0-0-0	12	100.0	10	62.4	9	36.0	4	25.0	1	11.1
B 0-0-1	0	0.0	5	31.3	8	32.0	6	37.4	1	11.1
C 0-1-0	0	0.0	0	0.0	1	4.0	1	6.3	1	11.1
D 0-1-1	0	0.0	1	6.3	7	28.0	5	31.3	6	66.7
Total	12	100.0	16	100.0	25	100.0	16	100.0	9	100.0

Table 33

Patterns of change in ego status with regard to the criterion of normalcy
(ego status 4 and 5): Wechsler Intelligence Scale
for Children Full IQ at admission

		WISC Full IQ at Admission			
		Below 70		70 & Over	
Criterion Pattern		Number	Per cent	Number	Per cent
A	0-0-0	22	78.6	14	28.0
B	0-0-1	5	17.9	15	30.0
C	0-1-0	0	0.0	3	6.0
D	0-1-1	1	3.6	18	36.0
	Total	28	100.1	50	100.0

the child's ego status at admission, the more likely it was for the child to attain mildly impaired to normal levels by discharge (ego levels 4 and 5).

As might be expected from our earlier remarks, this relation between ego status at admission and later outcome is less clear if placement at home or institution is used as a criterion of outcome (Table 37). Thus, much like the children with ego status ratings of 3, a majority of the children admitted to the residence with the lowest ego status ratings of 1 and 2 returned to their family on discharge. However, a very high proportion of the psychotic children (92.6%) admitted to the residence with ego status rating 3 and representing the highest order of children among the psychotic children, returned home on discharge. This was a significantly higher proportion returning home than shown by the children with lower ego status on admission so that placement at home at discharge was influenced by ego status at start of treatment.

The same pattern of relationship between adaptive competence at admission to treatment at approximately seven years of age and ego status outcome at discharge is demonstrated if WISC Full IQ at admission to treatment is employed as a criterion of initial integrative level (Table 38). Here it can be seen that there was a clear cut and consistent rise in percentage of children who attained mildly impaired to normal levels of ego status (ego levels 4, 5) when the admission IQ was high and, of course, an equally consistent rise in percentage of children who remained grossly impaired in levels of ego status (ego levels 1, 2, 3) when the admission IQ was low. None of the children with initial IQs below 46, that is with functional capacities so low that they were unmeasurable on the WISC, attained mildly impaired to normal levels of ego organization. Only one child (6.2%) among those with WISC Full IQs between 46 and 69 attained such mildly impaired to normal levels.

Table 34

Patterns of change in placement with regard to the criterion of normalcy
(home placement): Wechsler Intelligence Scale for Children Full IQ at admission

| | WISC FULL IQ at Admission | | | | | | | | | |
| | Below 46 | | 46–69 | | 70–89 | | 90–109 | | 110 & Above | |
Criterion Pattern	Number	Per cent	Number	Per cent	Number	Per cent	Number	Per cent	Number	Per cent
A 0-0-0	5	41.7	2	12.5	3	12.0	0	0.0	0	0.0
B 0-0-1	0	0.0	3	18.8	2	8.0	2	12.5	0	0.0
C 0-1-0	4	33.3	4	25.0	1	4.0	3	18.8	0	0.0
D 0-1-1	3	25.0	7	43.8	19	76.0	11	68.8	9	100.0
Total	12	100.0	16	100.1	25	100.0	16	100.1	9	100.0

Table 35

Patterns of change in placement with regard to the criterion of
normalcy (home placement): Wechsler Intelligence Scale for Children
Full IQ at admission

| | | WISC FULL IQ at Admission | | | |
| | | Below 70 | | 70 & Over | |
Criterion Pattern		Number	Per cent	Number	Per cent
A	0-0-0	7	25.0	3	6.0
B	0-0-1	3	10.7	4	8.0
C	0-1-0	8	28.6	4	8.0
D	0-1-1	10	35.7	39	78.0
	Total	28	100.0	50	100.0

Table 36

Ego status at discharge from residential treatment and at
admission to residential treatment

| | Ego Status at Admission | | | | | |
| | Level 1 | | Level 2 | | Level 3 | |
Ego Status at Discharge	Number	Per cent	Number	Per cent	Number	Per cent
Mildly Impaired to Normal	0	0.0	8	21.1	14	51.9
Grossly Impaired	13	100.0	30	78.9	13	48.1
Total	13	100.0	38	100.0	27	100.0

Table 37

Placement at discharge and ego status at admission to
residential treatment

| | Ego Status at Admission | | | | | |
| | Level 1 | | Level 2 | | Level 3 | |
Placement at Discharge	Number	Per cent	Number	Per cent	Number	Per cent
Home	9	69.2	26	68.4	25	92.6
Institution	4	30.8	12	31.6	2	7.4
Total	13	100.0	38	100.0	27	100.0

However, significant proportions of children with WISC Full IQs of 70
and above (44.0%) improved to mildly impaired or normal ego levels
enabling the children to contend with ordinary family and community
life. Indeed, a majority (56.0%) of children with normal IQs (90 or
higher) reached mildly impaired to normal levels of ego status by
discharge.

Table 38

Ego status at discharge from residential treatment and Wechsler Intelligence Scale
for Children Full IQ at admission

	WISC Full IQ at Admission								
	Below 46		46–69		70–89		90–109		110 & above	
Ego Status at Discharge	Number	Per cent	Number	Per cent	Number	Per cent	Number	Per cent	Number	Per cent
Mildly Impaired to Normal	0	0.0	1	6.2	8	32.0	7	43.8	7	77.8
Grossly Impaired	12	100.0	15	93.8	17	68.0	9	56.2	2	22.2
Total	12	100.0	16	100.0	25	100.0	16	100.0	9	100.0

Again, home placement at discharge is found in the majority of children at each IQ level (Table 39). There is, nevertheless, a direct association between home placement and IQ at admission.

As at discharge from residential treatment, social and psychiatric outcome at last follow-up was strongly associated with the child's ego status at admission to residential treatment (Table 40). Thus only one of 13 children (7.7%) classified at admission at lowest level of ego organization (ego level 1) attained mildly impaired to normal ego levels at follow-up. A higher proportion (39.5%) of children at level 2 in ego status at admission and a much higher percentage (81.5%) of children at level 3 in ego status at admission reached mildly impaired to normal levels of ego organization at follow-up. The contrast between the most impaired children at admission (ego level 1) and the remainder of the children (ego levels 2, 3) in extent of individual normalization in ego organization is dramatic and very significant. In a similar fashion ego status at admission is positively associated with placement at follow-up (Table 41). Thus, children who, at 7.2 years of age were at lowest levels of ego organization when they were admitted to treatment, also showed a lower percentage of subjects at home on follow-up at 19.9 years than those who, on beginning treatment, were categorized at the higher levels of ego organization (that is, ego levels 2 and 3).

The children's response to intelligence testing at admission to residential treatment was also unequivocally associated with ego status at follow-up (Table 42). When the children were distributed by WISC Full IQ at admission, those with higher IQs consistently showed a higher percentage of children attaining normal levels of ego organization (ego levels 4, 5) at last follow-up than children with lower IQs. For example, all the children whose intellectual functioning was so low that they were unmeasurable on the Wechsler Intelligence Scale for Children were still grossly impaired at last follow-up. This finding contrasted sharply with outcomes at follow-up of children who were scorable on the WISC, since a majority of these scorable children (59.1%) attained near normal to normal levels of ego organization. Sixty-eight percent of children with IQs 70 and above achieved such normal levels of ego organization. Of great interest is the fact that 72.0% of children with at least normal IQs (90 and above) and 77.8% of children with IQs of 110 and over achieved mildly impaired to normal ego status at follow-up.

Similarly, only 25% of the unscorable children in intelligence testing were to be found living at home at follow-up (Table 43). Seventy-five percent of these children were in institutions for the emotionally disturbed or mentally retarded at follow-up. In sharp contrast, 80.3% of the scorable children were living at home.

Table 39

Placement at discharge from residential treatment and Wechsler Intelligence Scale
for Children Full IQ at Admission

Placement at Discharge	WISC Full IQ at Admission									
	Below 46		46–69		70–89		90–109		110 & above	
	Number	Per cent	Number	Per cent	Number	Per cent	Number	Per cent	Number	Per cent
Home	7	58.3	11	68.7	20	80.0	14	87.5	9	100.0
Institution	5	41.7	5	31.3	5	20.0	2	12.5	0	0.0
Total	12	100.0	16	100.0	25	100.0	16	100.0	9	100.0

Table 40

Ego status at last follow-up and at admission to
residential treatment

	Ego Status at Admission					
	Level 1		Level 2		Level 3	
Ego Status at last follow-up	Number	Per cent	Number	Per cent	Number	Per cent
Mildly Impaired to Normal	1	7.7	15	39.5	22	81.5
Grossly Impaired	12	92.3	23	60.5	5	18.5
Total	13	100.0	38	100.0	27	100.0

Table 41

Placement at last follow-up and ego status at admission
to residential treatment

	Ego Status at Admission					
	Level 1		Level 2		Level 3	
Placement at last Follow-up	Number	Per cent	Number	Per cent	Number	Per cent
Home	5	38.5	27	71.1	24	88.9
Institution	8	61.5	11	28.9	3	11.1
Total	13	100.0	38	100.0	27	100.0

Outcomes in adolescence and later maturity may also be linked profitably to ego status at discharge from residential treatment (Table 44). All children who were still grossly impaired in ego (at the lowest ego levels 1 and 2) at discharge remained at grossly impaired levels at follow-up. The only children to attain mildly impaired to normal ego levels at follow-up had been at ego levels 3 or 4 on discharge. Placement at follow-up was also associated significatnly with ego status at discharge (Table 45).

Sex

Lotter (1974) has noted in his group of autistic children that girls uniformly showed poor social outcomes. In fact, in his group, no instances of good or fair outcome were found among the girls. He also noted supportive data for better outcome in boys in follow-up appraisals of other samples of psychotic children (Bender, 1970; DeMyer, 1973; Rutter et al, 1967).

At the Ittleson Center, as well, a number of studies have demonstrated that the girls tended to be lower than boys in such measures of

Table 42

Ego status at last follow-up and Wechsler Intelligence Scale for Children
Full IQ at admission

| | WISC Full IQ at Admission | | | | | | | | | |
| | Below 46 | | 46—69 | | 70—89 | | 90—109 | | 110 & above | |
Ego Status at last Follow-up	Number	Per cent	Number	Per cent	Number	Per cent	Number	Per cent	Number	Per cent
Mildly impaired to Normal	0	0.0	5	31.3	16	64.0	11	68.7	7	77.8
Grossly impaired	12	100.0	11	68.7	9	36.0	5	31.3	2	22.2
Total	12	100.0	16	100.0	25	100.0	16	100.0	9	100.0

Table 43

Placement at last follow-up and Wechsler Intelligence Scale for Children
Full IQ at admission

| | WISC Full IQ At Admission | | | | | | | | | |
| | Below 46 | | 46—69 | | 70—89 | | 90—109 | | 110 & above | |
Placement at last Follow-up	Number	Per cent	Number	Per cent	Number	Per cent	Number	Per cent	Number	Per cent
Home	3	25.0	10	62.5	21	84.0	13	81.3	9	100.0
Institution	9	75.0	6	37.5	4	16.0	3	18.7	0	0.0
Total	12	100.0	16	100.0	25	100.0	16	100.0	9	100.0

Table 44

Ego status at last follow-up and ego status at discharge from treatment

| | Ego Status at Discharge | | | | | | | |
| | Level 1 | | Level 2 | | Level 3 | | Level 4 | |
Ego status at last Follow-up	Number	Per cent	Number	Per cent	Number	Per cent	Number	Per cent
Mildly impaired to normal	0	0.0	0	0.0	19	52.8	19	86.4
Grossly impaired	7	100.0	13	100.0	17	47.2	3	13.6
Total	7	100.0	13	100.0	36	100.0	22	100.0

Table 45

Placement at last follow-up and ego status at discharge from treatment

| | Ego Status at Discharge | | | | | | | |
| | Level 1 | | Level 2 | | Level 3 | | Level 4 | |
Placement at last Follow-up	Number	Per cent	Number	Per cent	Number	Per cent	Number	Per cent
Home	1	14.3	6	46.2	28	77.8	20	90.9
Institution	6	85.7	7	53.8	8	22.2	2	9.1
Total	7	100.0	13	100.0	36	100.0	22	100.0

adaptive function as IQ and school achievement (Goldfarb & Pollack, 1964; Goldfarb, Goldfarb & Pollack, 1969; Goldfarb, 1974). When measured with an extensive battery of tests, most significant differences tended to favor the boys (Goldfarb, 1974). Thus, boys exceeded girls in general orientation, verbal capacity (WISC VIQ), language communication and arithmetic attainment. Girls were superior in only one cognitive test, that is, the Weigl Test which measured the ability to categorize objects on the basis of color and shape, and in neurological tests of balance. Boys also tended to hold on to their cognitive superiority so that, for example, after three years of treatment boys were still superior in the measures of competence noted above.

However, a previous study of psychiatric and social outcomes (Goldfarb, 1970) has demonstrated that boys and girls, in an Ittleson Center sample of psychotic children, did not differ in percent who attained mildly impaired to normal levels of ego by discharge and at later follow-up and in percent living with their families in the community at these times. This finding of no significant difference between the boys and girls in psychiatric ratings of ego at discharge from residential treatment and at follow-up held when boys and girls were matched for ego status and neurological integrity at start of residential treatment.

Employing our present technique of classifying individual children by profiles of change on a criterion of normalcy, boys and girls did not differ significantly from each other in patterns of ego status changes (Table 46). Nor did they differ significantly in placement histories (Table

Table 46

Patterns of change in ego status with regard to the
criterion of normalcy (ego status 4 and 5): male and female

		Male		Female	
Criterion Pattern		Number	Per cent	Number	Per cent
A	0-0-0	28	47.5	9	47.4
B	0-0-1	12	20.3	7	36.8
C	0-1-0	3	5.1	0	0.0
D	0-1-1	16	27.1	3	15.8
	Total	59	100.0	19	100.0

47). When viewed at specific points in time, the boys and girls did not differ significantly at discharge and at follow-up in percent reaching mildly impaired to normal levels of ego (Tables 48, 50) and in percent returning home (Tables 49, 51).

Table 47

Patterns of change in placement with regard to the criterion
of normalcy (home placement): male and female

		Male		Female	
Criterion Pattern		Number	Per cent	Number	Per cent
A	0-0-0	7	11.9	3	15.8
B	0-0-1	5	8.5	3	15.8
C	0-1-0	11	18.6	1	5.3
D	0-1-1	36	61.0	12	63.2
	Total	59	100.0	19	100.1

Table 48

Ego status at discharge and sex

	Male		Female	
Ego Status at Discharge	Number	Per cent	Number	Per cent
Mildly Impaired to Normal	19	32.2	3	15.8
Grossly Impaired	40	67.8	16	84.2
Total	59	100.0	19	100.0

Table 49

Placement at discharge and sex

	Male		Female	
Placement at discharge	Number	Per cent	Number	Per cent
Home	47	79.7	13	68.4
Institution	12	20.3	6	31.6
Total	59	100.0	19	100.0

Table 50

Ego status at last follow-up and sex

	Male		Female	
Ego status at last Follow-up	Number	Per cent	Number	Per cent
Mildly impaired to normal	28	47.5	10	52.6
Grossly impaired	31	52.5	9	47.4
Total	59	100.0	19	100.0

Table 51

Placement at last follow-up and sex

Placement at last Follow-up	Male		Female	
	Number	Per cent	Number	Per cent
Home	41	69.5	15	78.9
Institution	18	30.5	4	21.1
Total	59	100.0	19	100.0

The finding of no significant differences between boys and girls in ego status and in proportion at home at discharge and at last follow-up is also supported when the 19 girls are matched with 19 boys for ego status at admission and for neurological integrity (Tables 52 to 55).

Table 52

Ego status at discharge of boys and girls, matched in neurological status and in ego status at admission

Ego Status at Discharge	Male		Female	
	Number	Per cent	Number	Per cent
Mildly impaired to normal	9	47.4	3	15.8
Grossly impaired	10	52.6	16	84.2
Total	19	100.0	19	100.0

Table 53

Placement at discharge of boys and girls, matched in neurological status and in ego status at admission

Placement at Discharge	Male		Female	
	Number	Per cent	Number	Per cent
Home	13	68.4	12	63.2
Institution	6	31.6	7	36.8
Total	19	100.0	19	100.0

Age of admission to residential treatment

Since early onset of their developmental disorders was characteristic of all the children, age of onset was not employed as a distinguishing independent variable. However, we have previously demonstrated the profit in subdividing the children by age of admission to

Table 54

Ego status at last follow-up of boys and girls, matched in
neurological status and in ego status at admission

Ego Status at last Follow-up	Male		Female	
	Number	Per cent	Number	Per cent
Mildly impaired to normal	7	36.8	10	52.6
Grossly impaired	12	63.2	9	47.4
Total	19	100.0	19	100.0

Table 55

Placement at last follow-up of boys and girls, matched in
neurological status and in ego status at admission

Placement at last Follow-up	Male		Female	
	Number	Per cent	Number	Per cent
Home	11	57.9	14	73.7
Institution	8	42.1	5	26.3
Total	19	100.0	19	100.0

treatment (Goldfarb, 1974). Thus, children in the present population
who were admitted to residential treatment below eight years of age were
different from children admitted at eight years of age or older. For
example, the older children came from families who were lower in social
class position. In addition, all the most extremely impaired children who
were unmeasurable in the Wechsler Scale came from the younger age
group. These children also tended strongly to belong to the organic
subgroup of children. Finally, the two subclasses of children, defined by
age of admission to treatment, differed in their longitudinal curves of
change during treatment. When measured in a large variety of measures
of purposeful function, the older children were superior at admission to
treatment and each subsequent year of treatment in most measures,
with only a few exceptions.

In the present study, when the children are subdivided by admission age, analysis of patterns of change in ego status, utilizing our
criterion of normalcy, shows no significant difference between older and
younger children (Table 56). However, the two groups of children did
differ in pattern of change when the criterion of normalcy referred to
home placement (Table 57). In other words, for home placement, a
higher percent of the younger children presented pattern A, in which
there is no significant improvement in both treatment and follow-up

Table 56

Patterns of change in ego status with regard to the criterion
of normalcy (ego status 4 and 5): age at admission to treatment

		Age at Admission			
		Below 8 Years		8 Years & Older	
Criterion Pattern		Number	Per cent	Number	Per cent
A	0-0-0	21	53.8	16	41.0
B	0-0-1	11	28.2	8	20.5
C	0-1-0	1	2.6	2	5.1
D	0-1-1	6	15.4	13	33.3
	Total	39	100.0	39	99.9

Table 57

Patterns of change in placement with regard to the criterion
of normalcy (home placement): age at admission to treatment

		Age at Admission			
		Below 8 Years		8 Years & Older	
Criterion Pattern		Number	Per cent	Number	Per cent
A	0-0-0	8	20.5	3	7.7
B	0-0-1	7	17.9	1	2.6
C	0-1-0	7	17.9	5	12.8
D	0-1-1	17	43.6	30	76.9
	Total	39	99.9	39	100.0

periods; and the older children show a higher percent of children who attain pattern D, in which the child attained normalcy by time of discharge from treatment and maintained his gains in follow-up.

Examination of the children's status cross-sectionally demonstrates that more of the older children attained mildly impaired to normal levels of ego and were at home at discharge from treatment (Tables 58, 59). However, by last follow-up, the two age subgroups did not differ in regard to both ego status and placement criteria of normalcy (Tables 60, 61).

SUMMARY OF FINDINGS

Seventy-eight psychotic children, treated by an extensive complement of therapeutic services embodied in residential treatment at the Ittleson Center for Child Research between 1953 and

Table 58

Ego status at discharge and age of admission to
residential treatment

	Age at Admission			
	Below 8 Years		8 Years & Older	
Ego Status at Discharge	Number	Per cent	Number	Per cent
Mildly impaired to normal	7	18.0	15	38.5
Grossly impaired	32	82.0	24	61.5
Total	39	100.0	39	100.0

Table 59

Placement at discharge and age of admission to residential
treatment

	Age at Admission			
	Below 8 Years		8 Years & Older	
Placement at Discharge	Number	Per cent	Number	Per cent
Home	24	61.5	35	89.7
Institution	15	38.5	4	10.3
Total	39	100.0	39	100.0

Table 60

Ego status at last follow-up and age of admission to
residential treatment

	Age at Admission			
	Below 8 Years		8 Years & Older	
Ego Status at last follow-up	Number	Per cent	Number	Per cent
Mildly impaired to normal	17	43.6	21	53.9
Grossly impaired	22	56.4	18	46.2
Total	39	100.0	39	100.0

Table 61

Placement at last follow-up and age of admission to
residential treatment

	Age at Admission			
	Below 8 Years		8 Years & Older	
Placement at last Follow-up	Number	Per cent	Number	Per cent
Home	24	61.5	31	79.5
Institution	15	38.5	8	20.5
Total	39	100.0	39	100.0

1969, were studied in a prospective longitudinal fashion while in treatment and during subsequent follow-up. They were appraised globally in terms of ego status at admission to residential treatment at a mean age of 7.2 years, at discharge at a mean age of 11.2 years and at last follow-up at a mean age of 19.9 years. The total period of observation was an average of 12.7 years. Employing criteria of normalcy based on psychiatric ratings of ego and on placement course, each child's longitudinal course was classified in terms of profile or pattern of change. In addition, group trends at admission, discharge from treatment and at last follow-up were summarized.

At discharge, 76.9% of the children were discharged home to their families; and, while specific areas of functional improvement have been noted in virtually all the children, 28.2% reached levels of mildly impaired to normal levels of global ego organization, reflected in capacity to adjust to the demands of community (school, job) and family living with an ordinary expectable degree of autonomy.

At follow-up 8.7 years after discharge from residential treatment, 71.8% were still living at home and now 48.7% of the children had reached mildly impaired to normal levels of ego integration.

A significant number of the children showed sufficient improvement in ego status in the course of residential treatment to attain mildly impaired to normal levels of ego integration. Perhaps, even more strikingly, a significant number of additional children continued to improve and to attain such non-psychotic, near normal levels of ego after discharge from treatment. If we consider the three points of evaluation in the longitudinal observation—admission to residential treatment in early childhood, discharge from residential treatment and last follow-up—all the children were psychotic and most grossly impaired in ego at admission to treatment, they were less impaired at discharge, and least impaired in follow-up 12.7 years after the first observation. The individual children showed varying patterns of change.

No child declined in ego status while in treatment. In the follow-up period, 8.7 years after discharge from treatment, three children who had attained mildly impaired to normal levels in residential treatment showed declines in ego organization and acute psychotic decompensations. However, in the same period, 21 children had emerged from psychotic levels of ego organization to near normal levels.

Factors appraised for association with ultimate outcome included neurological integrity, socio-economic position of the family, ego status (including IQ) of the child at admission to treatment, ego status at discharge from treatment, sex of the child and age of admission to treatment.

A. Neurological integrity of child

At discharge from treatment, children who were free of evidence of neurological dysfunction in their neurological histories and examinations (non-organic children) at the start of residential treatment were superior to children who presented evidence of neurological dysfunction (organic children). That is, proportionately more of the non-organic children attained near normal to normal levels in ego status by the time they were discharged from the residence. However, this difference between organic and non-organic children in social and psychiatric outcome, as expressed in psychiatric ratings of ego status, disappeared in the follow-up period. As in a previous investigation, organic children were more inclined to hold the gains they had attained by the end of residential treatment. (All three instances of decompensation to psychotic levels of ego from normal levels at discharge from treatment were non-organic boys.)

B. Socio-economic position (Hollingshead-Redlich Index of Social Position)

Our studies have presented evidence of differences in levels of adaptive competence among psychotic children of different social classes. Specifically, these investigations demonstrated an inverse relationship between measures of adaptive competence of the children (e.g. IQ) and the socio-economic class of the families. However, using the summative judgments embodied in the psychiatric ratings of ego status, no significant class differences can be discerned in the present study at discharge from treatment or follow-up in percent of children who attained mildly impaired to normal levels. Similarly, there was no difference among socio-economic classes in percent of children sent home at discharge. More children from poor families, however, were living at home at later follow-up.

C. Ego status at admission

This variable is shown to be the major dimension associated with outcome at discharge from treatment and, again at follow-up. With rare exception, psychotic children at the very lowest levels of ego organization (ego status 1) who demonstrated the most extreme deficiencies in attachment behavior, language, self-awareness, perceptual receptivity, cognition and educational response were still grossly impaired in ego at discharge from treatment and again at later follow-up in adolescence and adulthood. In contrast, a majority of psychotic children with highest levels of ego organization (ego status 3) in the psychotic universe attained mildly impaired to normal levels of ego integration (ego levels 4, 5) at discharge from treatment and an even higher percent of these children attained such levels of adaptive response by last follow-up. Children in the middle range of ego organization within the psychotic group fell between the children at the two extremes in ego organization at discharge from treatment and, later, at follow up.

D. Ego status at discharge

In considering criteria for prediction of outcome at last follow-up, it is also important to note that all children who remained at the two lowest levels of ego (ego levels 1, 2) at discharge also remained grossly impaired at follow-up. In contrast, the great bulk of children who had attained either ego level 3, the highest level of ego organization within the psychotic range of children, or ego level 4, characterized by mild impairment of ego, were to be found at mildly impaired to normal ranges of ego organization and to be living at home at follow-up.

E. Sex

Boys and girls did not differ significantly in ego level and placement course at discharge from treatment and later at follow-up.

F. Age of admission to residential treatment

More of the children entering treatment at eight years or over showed improvement to mildly impaired to normal ego levels and were sent home at discharge from the residence than did children below eight years at admission; but these differences did not hold in follow-up

DISCUSSION

One may approach the therapeutic care and management of psychotic children with the optimistic certainty that there is a distinct trend to improvement and growth in these children. They all begin life as highly deviant children with massive irregularities and deficits in the emergent latticework of their personalities. In a sense, among the behavior disorders they are the most conspicuous examples of developmental lag. However, as they become older, the group trend is clearly toward adaptive and functional normalization (Goldfarb, 1970, 1974). Thus, in a broad sample of psychotic children who have all been clearly deviant from the earliest months of life, the prevalence of patent psychosis may be expected to diminish as the children grow older, pass through adolescence and enter early adulthood. (This trend among psychotic children, of course, stands in contrast to that noted in children at high genetic risk for adult schizophrenia during the period between adolescence and the middle adult years.)

However, the rate of improvement in ego status of psychotic children is slow, indeed. At the Ittleson Center, psychotic children were offered residential treatment for as long as clinical judgment indicated that they or their families required it or until the residence was no longer feasible. Under these circumstances the mean duration of treatment was 4.0 years. At this point, while 76.9% returned home, only 28.2% of the children had reached mildly impaired to normal levels of ego as defined in our scale of ego status. And it was not till follow-up at 19.9 years that 48.7% of the children reached mildly impaired to normal levels of ego organization. In addition, at some time in the follow-up interval, all of the children required one or another kind of counseling, therapy or special educational accommodation, regardless of level of ego organization attained. Of the 58 children sent home on discharge, some form of social service was provided to 51 (88%) of the children. At last follow-up, 41 of the 53 subjects living at home (77.4%) were still receiving active psychiatric, social or educational service. Thus, these children have all needed a significant degree of supportive service throughout childhood and adolescence.

While it may be administratively expedient to provide only very brief and attenuated forms of therapy for psychotic children, such forms of therapy do not reflect their needs as shown by the rate and pattern of change in these children. Base line longitudinal studies, such as the present one, would support a design for the therapeutic management of the psychotic child which encompasses all of childhood and adolescence and which makes flexible and differential use of services varying in intensity and complexity throughout this period.

A major intrusion in the normal life course of the children of the present study was deliberately provided during their prolonged placement in a residence away from their families in their early school years. During this long period between about seven and eleven years of age, a conscious effort was made to surround the children with a therapeutic milieu; that is to say, to foster ego growth by enhancing experiences throughout the 24 hours of the day for each of the children. In doing so, we were most immediately conscious of the therapeutic challenge posed by the distortions and gaps in the development of the children. However, we were also strongly responsive to and identified with the families of the children—their parents and siblings as individuals and their families as functional units. We were keenly aware of their intense urgency and despair as well as the peaking sense of failure on the part of the larger community. We encouraged the parents to assume primary responsibility for the application for placement; and expended great effort in the clarification of parental ambivalence. Generally speaking, these parents consciously wanted to remain in the picture and were drawn selectively to a therapeutic program for psychotic children which emphasized its concern for the parents.

While we linked the child's admission and the subsequent residential program to his psychiatric classification as psychotic, we understood from the beginning that his ultimate discharge need not be so unequivocally determined by his clinical diagnosis. Children were to be maintained in residence so long as we judged that their stay in the residence facilitated progress in the families and the children. Using broad criteria reflecting the child's social competence and therapeutic needs, children were also to be discharged when the children possessed the attributes needed for re-entry into the community and would benefit from such re-entry, regardless of psychopathologic classification. Discharge was unquestionably justified in the case of all children who had attained near normal to normal levels of ego competence. However, it also seemed warranted in the case of some children who had achieved a level of social competence which enabled them to live in the community despite the fact that careful psychiatric assay supported their continued classification as psychotic and grossly impaired in ego. In actual empirical fact, with few exceptions, virtually all children who had reached mildly impaired to normal levels by time of discharge from the residence did return home. In addition, however, a large proportion of children still considered to be grossly impaired in ego competence returned home.

We have knowingly discharged children from the treatment program who had not as yet emerged from psychotic levels of ego integration when it seemed to us that they had made sufficient progress so that they could live in the community despite the psychiatric diagnosis; and we also did so in the optimistic hope that the impetus to improvement initiated in residential care would continue after discharge. Frequently, it seemed to us that even while still psychotic the child had attained an inner ideal of normalcy and was reaching for its fulfillment. In addition, it was frequently our judgment that this crucial passage into normalcy demanded that the child leave the institution and enter the larger community where normal behavior was more expected and abnormal behavior was more explicitly discouraged. To sustain his normal ideal, so to speak, he needed the enhancing stimulation of the normal environment.

It would appear to be inconsistent that children who had been admitted to residential treatment because they were demonstrating severe psychotic impairment were often discharged from residential treatment despite the continuing evidence of childhood psychosis. Indeed, case analysis revealed that the latter group of children did include some children for whom home placement was patently a doubtful plan and who were brought home at parental insistence. A number of these children were transferred eventually to institutions for the emotionally disturbed. However, the group also included some children with evidence of sustained continuing improvement after discharge from residential treatment.

Empirical support for the discharge back to the community of a proportion of the children who were still grossly impaired in ego is to be found in the follow-up observations. In this regard, a finding of great significance was the number of children who attained mildly impaired to normal levels of ego only after leaving the residential treatment center. While 28.2% of the children had reached about near normal levels of ego integration in residential treatment, an additional 20.5% did so in follow-up after leaving the treatment center.

The present investigation underscores the key significance of the child's level of ego organization in defining severity of functional impairment within the universe of psychotic children and, most pertinently in this report, in predicting ultimate clinical and social outcomes in adolescence and adulthood. All the criteria for the diagnosis of early childhood psychosis reflect developmental impairments in the child's self regulative conduct, manifested in the first two to three years of life. These deficits in pattern and level of ego organization refer to a whole gamut of purposeful functions, including perception, conceptualization, psychomotor ability and language, and also to social relationships and affective response. In every instance one observes deviant response to humans, disordered communication, panic in the face of change or novelty and a concurrent disposition towards all kinds of ritualistic, perservative and echoic behaviors.

However, implicit in the approach to diagnosis and evaluation of change through the assay of self regulative behavior is the awareness of the very broad range of functional impairments among the individual children in the universe of children classified as psychotic. Indeed, as noted, the individual psychotic child's ego level, which defines his level of clinical impairment, correlates highly with or, perhaps, even determines his ultimate clinical and social outcomes in later life. We have long been aware that individual pattern and level of ego organization rather than the mere diagnosis of psychosis should determine the design of therapeutic and remedial programs. Our findings now make it clear that the child's level of ego can be used to predict later clinical and social outcomes more powerfully than the mere diagnosis of childhood psychosis. With the very high association of ego level with ultimate clinical and social outcome and the weaker association between outcome and other independent variables, such as sex, neurological status and social class, we have also observed multivariate approaches to estimates of outcome based on the combined use of these variables do not significantly improve upon the predictive value of ego level alone.

In designing operational tools for the assay of ego status, one has the choice of global judgments which summate observations of many facets of adaptive responses or of focused assays of more delineated and more precisely defined areas of competence. Examples of global judgments include our own ratings of ego status by psychiatrists in the present study or ranking of the children with regard to "normality" or proximity to the presumptive normal by all members of the professional staff in a previous study (Goldfarb, 1961). Examples of more precisely defined purposeful functions which have been evaluated by systematic test and observation include intelligence, psychomotor ability, social maturity and language.

In planning tools for a longitudinal study of clinical and social outcomes in childhood psychosis, we have been impressed by the overlap among appraisal procedures, an overlap confirmed by factor analysis of test and observational scores (Goldfarb, 1961). In this study, we have used a global rating of ego status in assaying follow-up changes, inasmuch as this rating summated numerous and relevant observations of the child in his world, embodied in clinical and therapeutic experience with a child. At the same time, we have observed the association of outcome in follow-up with other measures of adaptive competence such as IQ and language competence (Goldfarb, 1970). Our findings, therefore, agree with those of other observers who have reported a correlation between a variety of measures of adaptive level in childhood and ultimate outcomes.

Recently, the correlation of IQ with outcome has been particularly stressed in follow-up appraisal (Bartak & Rutter, 1976; DeMyer et al, 1974; Goldfarb, 1970; Lotter, 1974). We have been impressed with the power of a measure which presumably features cognitive competence to predict outcome in a disorder which encompasses emotional and social as well as cognitive features. Here we need to remind ourselves that the IQ in itself reflects the emotional as well as cognitive correlates of childhood psychosis and that it indeed overlaps with other measures of "normality" (Goldfarb, 1961). On the other hand, if one assumes a threshhold for the diagnosis of gross social and clinical normalcy, it is conceivable that the child is brought over this threshhold by attributes such as high IQ and educational attainment even when certain social and emotional features remain grossly aberrant. Such discordance between intellectual or educational competence and emotional integration is frequently to be noted.

If, as in the present investigation, one studies a broad array of psychotic children in early childhood and until they reach adulthood, one is in a position to test the predictive power of early observations. In the past, in the course of treating the children as individuals, we have found ourselves relatively uninterested in making predictions at the start of treatment and have rather approached each child with a strong and optimistic therapeutic intention. However, predictions are of obvious merit for the public health planner in designing and selecting the variety and the differential use of services which are needed for psychotic children. Our studies have tended to bring into relief the predictive power of the psychotic child's primary or residual adaptive competence in the early school years. We feel confident we shall confirm in a new group of children the high predictability of outcome in the instance of children at the extremes of capacity in early childhood, even though they do change a great deal. It will be recalled, for example, that in testing the association between outcome and multiple variables we found that children at lowest levels of ego status at admission (ego level 1) did not ever attain mildly impaired to normal levels of ego at discharge and rarely (7.7%) at later follow-up; and children at lowest, unmeasurable IQ levels (below IQ 46) never attained mildly impaired to normal levels of adjustment at discharge and follow-up. In contrast, children at highest levels of ego within the psychotic universe (ego level 3) showed a distinct trend to normalization, since 51.9% at discharge and 81.5% at follow-up evidenced mildly impaired to normal ego competence. Similarly, of children with IQs 70 or over, 44.0% at discharge and 68.0% at follow-up reached near normal levels. Of children with IQs 90 or over, 56.0% at discharge and 72.0% at follow-up attained near normal levels of ego competence.

We have been concerned with the changing needs of the children for institutional management as the subjects became older. For example, while it was our judgment that institutional treatment was advisable for all the children at admission to treatment, approximately three-fourths of the children were sent home at discharge at the average age of 11.2 years and approximatley the same ratio were in the community at follow-up 8.7 years later. Empirically, we found that after discharge, most plans for renewed institutional care were restricted to children at lowest levels of ego integration who from the beginning were most restricted in language, intelligence and capacity for self care. Their lifelong custodial needs emerged in sharper relief as they entered adolescence and their maturity. Further, whereas the clinical objective in institutional placement in the early school years was therapeutic and indeed represented an effort to expose the child to comprehensive round-the-clock treatment, after discharge, institutionalization more frequently reflected a desperate family and community need for a custodial arrangement for the child who was extremely impaired and unresponsive.

We are reminded of a previous study comparing day and residential services for the psychotic child (Goldfarb, 1970). This study supported the conclusion that organic psychotic children of early school age responded equally well to treatment in day and residential programs; but that the non-organic children tended to respond better to the 24 hour program of the residence. (This study, too, is now in the follow-up phase of longitudinal study). The conclusions of the day versus residence study are consonant with our emerging clinical judgment that the therapeutic residence in the early school years is most suitable as a clinical tool for the affirmative treatment of the non-organic child, in whom neurological considerations are insignificant, who has normal capacities, and who appears to be struggling with conspicuous social, familial and intrapsychic stresses. These stresses are most effectively alleviated while the child is separated from his family. As noted in the present study, a majority of such children improve in the treatment regimen of the residence. Although still awaiting systematic appraisal, it is our present conviction, therefore, that early institutional care should be utilized for the active treatment of the higher order child who may benefit from an interval of separation from the family environment. Later, in adolescence, institutional care appears more suitably reserved for the psychotic children at lower levels of ego integration, who are increasingly difficult to manage as they attain adulthood. In a related sense, institutional care in adolescence or later is more strongly linked to the mental deficiency of the psychotic child than it was in the earlier years, when psychodynamic and interpersonal factors were influential determinants in the plans for institutionalization.

At the outset, we suggested that the longitudinal study of early childhood psychosis provides a powerful tool for observing a link between early childhood psychopathology and that of adulthood. In this regard, such longitudinal study has much to contribute to considerations pertaining to the process-reactive continuum hypothesized in adult schizophrenia (Kantor & Herron, 1966). Here, reference is made to the concept of the "poor premorbid-good premorbid" dichotomy, pragmatically derived from quantification of mental status and case history data and their correlation with recovery. The poor premorbid patient has been distinguished on the basis of early onset, absence of an apparent precipitant, and poor outcome; and the good premorbid patient on the basis of later onset, acute onset often with clear precipitant and good outcome. There is a current trend to believe that the poor premorbid cases reflect organic etiology and the good premorbid cases reflect psychogenic etiology. Linked strongly to this concept is the belief that the poor premorbid can come to no good end. Our data provide a test of this belief since children with early childhood psychosis do represent the most extreme instances of "poor premorbidity"; and therefore the most extreme therapeutic challenges. Careful, detailed clinical study of the Ittleson Center children in course of development elicits episodic variations in behavior, including rises and falls, which are reasonably correlated with specific social and psychological antecedents. Generally, we have found social and psychiatric outcomes are impressively favorable, provided the child possesses an expectable and sufficient degree of cerebral potential and provided a range of supportive services are made available to him throughout his childhood.

REFERENCES

Annell, A.L. The prognosis of psychotic syndromes in children. *Acta Psychiatra Scandinavica*, 1963, *39*, 235-297.

Bartak, L. & Rutter, M. Differences between mentally retarded and normally intelligent autistic children. *Journal of Autism and Childhood Schizophrenia*, 1976, *6*, 109-120.

Bender, L. Childhood schizophrenia. *The Nervous Child*, 1941, *1*, 138-140.

Bender, L. Autism in children with mental deficiency. *American Journal of Mental Deficiency*, 1959, *63*(7), 81-86.

Bender, L. The life course of schizophrenic children. *Biological Psychiatry*, 1970, *2*, 165-172.

Bender, L., & Grugett, A.E., Jr. A study of certain epidemiological factors in a group of children with childhood schizophrenia. *American Journal of Orthopsychiatry*, 1956, *26*, 131.

Bennett, S. & Klein, H.R. Childhood schizophrenia: 30 years later. *American Journal of Psychiatry*, 1966, *122*, 1121-1124.

Bettelheim, B. *The empty fortress*. New York: The Free Press, 1967.

Brown, J.L. Prognosis from presenting symptoms of preschool children with atypical development. *American Journal of Orthopsychiatry*, 1960, *30*, 382-390.

Brown, J.L. Follow-up of children with atypical development (infantile psychosis). *American Journal of Orthopsychiatry*, 1963, *33*, 855-861.

Colbert, E.G. & Koegler, R.R. The childhood schizophrenic in adolescence. *Psychiatric Quarterly*, 1961, *35*, 693-701.

Creak, M. Schizophrenic syndrome in childhood. *Cerebral Palsy Bulletin*, 1961, *3*, 501.

Creak, M. Psychosis - a review of 100 cases. *British Journal of Psychiatry*, 1963, *109*, 84-89.

Davids, A., Ryan, R., & Salvatore, P.D. Effectiveness of residential treatment for psychotic and other disturbed children. *American Journal of Orthopsychiatry*, 1968, *38*, 469-475.

DeMyer, M.K., Barton, T., Alpern, G.D., Kimberlin, C., Allen, J., Yank, E., & Steele, R. The measured intelligence of autistic children. *Journal of Autism and Childhood Schizophrenia*, 1974, *4*(1), 42-60.

DeMyer, M.K., Barton, T., DeMyer, W.E., Norton, J.A., Allen, J., & Steele, R. Prognosis in autism: A follow-up study. *Journal of Autism and Childhood Schizophrenia*, 1973, *3*, 199-246.

Eaton, L. & Menolascino, F. *Psychotic reactions of childhood: A follow-up study*. Presented at the 1966 annual meeting of the American Orthopsychiatric Association, San Francisco, California, March 1966.

Eisenberg, L. The autistic child in adolescence. *American Journal of Psychiatry*, 1956, *12*, 607-613.

Eisenberg, L. The course of childhood schizophrenia. *Archives of Neurology and Psychiatry*, 1957, *78*, 69-83.

Fish, B., Shapiro, T., Campbell, M., & Wile, R. A classification of schizophrenic children under five years. *American Journal of Psychiatry*, 1968, *124*(10), 1415-1423.

Freedman, A.M. & Bender, L. When the childhood schizophrenic grows up. *American Journal of Orthopsychiatry*, 1957, *27*, 535-565.

Goldfarb, W. *Childhood schizophrenia*. Cambridge, Mass.: Harvard University Press, 1961.

Goldfarb, W. Childhood psychosis. In P.W. Mussen (Ed.) *Carmichael's Manual of Child Psychology*, New York: John Wiley & Sons, Inc., 1970.

Goldfarb, W. A follow-up investigation of schizophrenic children treated in residence. *Psychosocial Process*, 1970, *1*(1).

Goldfarb, W. *Growth and change of schizophrenic children: A longitudinal study*. Washington, D.C.: V.H. Winston & Sons, 1974.

Goldfarb, W., Goldfarb, N., & Pollack, R. A three year comparison of day and residential treatment of schizophrenic children. *Archives of General Psychiatry*, 1966, *14*, 119-128.

Goldfarb, W., Goldfarb, N., & Pollack, R. Changes in intelligence quotient of schizophrenic children during residential treatment. *Archives of General Psychiatry*, 1969, *21*, 673-690.

Goldfarb, W. & Pollack, R. The childhood schizophrenic's response to schooling in a residential treatment center. In P.H. Hoch & J. Zubin (Eds.), *The evaluation of psychiatric treatment*. New York: Grune & Stratton, 1964.

Hollingshead, A.B. & Redlich, F.C. *Social class and mental illness*. New York: John Wiley & Sons, 1958.

Kanner, L. Autistic disturbances of affective contact. *The Nervous Child*, 1943, *2*, 217-250.

Kanner, L. Problems of nosology and psychodynamics of early infantile autism. *American Journal of Orthopsychiatry*, 1949, *19*, 416-426.

Kanner, L. To what extent is early infantile autism determined by constitutional inadequacies? *Proceedings of the Association Res. Nervous & Mental Disease*, 1954, *33*, 378.

Kantor, R. & Herron, W. *Reactive process schizophrenia*. Palo Alto, California: Science and Behavior Books, Inc., 1966.

Kaufman, I., Frank, T., Friend, J., Heims, L.W., & Weiss, R. Success and failure in the treatment of childhood schizophrenia. *American Journal of Psychiatry*, 1962, *118*, 909-1015.

Lotter, V. Factors related to outcome in autistic children. *Journal of Autism and Childhood Schizophrenia*, 1974A, *4*(3), 263-277.

Lotter, V. Social outcome and placement of autistic children in Middlesex: A follow-up study. *Journal of Autism and Childhood Schizophrenia*, 1974B, *4*, 11-32.

Mahler, M.S. On child psychosis and schizophrenia: Autistic and symbiotic psychoses. *Psychoanalytic Study of Child*, 1952, *7*, 286-305.

Mahler, M.S. Autism and symbiosis: Two extreme disturbances of identity. *International Journal of Psychoanalysis*, 1958, *39* (Parts II-IV), 1-7.

Menolascino, F. Psychosis of childhood: Experiences of a mental retardation pilot project. *American Journal of Mental Deficiency*, 1965, *70*(1), 83-92.

Meyers, D.I. & Goldfarb, W. Psychiatric appraisals of parents and siblings of schizophrenic children. *American Journal of Psychiatry*, 1962, *118*, 902-908.

Potter, H.W. Schizophrenia in children. *American Journal of Psychiatry*, 1933, *12*(6), 1253-1270.

Reiser, D.E. & Brown, J.L. Patterns of later development in children with infantile psychosis. *Journal of the American Academy of Child Psychiatry*, 1964, *3*(4), 650-667.

Rimland, B. *Infantile autism*. London: Methuen, 1965.

Rutter, M. The influence of organic and emotional factors in the origins, nature and outcome of childhood psychosis. *Developmental Medicine and Child Neurology*, 1965, *7*, 518-528.

Rutter, M., Greenfield, D., & Lockyer, L. A five to fifteen year follow-up study of infantile psychosis: II. Social and behavioral outcome. *British Journal of Psychiatry*, 1967, *113*, 1183-1199.

Rutter, M. & Lockyer, L. A five to fifteen year follow-up study of infantile psychosis: I. Description of sample. *British Journal of Psychiatry*, 1967, *113*, 1109-1182.

DISCUSSION: THE OUTCOME OF INFANTILE PSYCHOSIS

Leon Eisenberg, M.D.*

In the 19th century, the global "diagnosis" of feeble-mindedness was employed without differentiation for a multitude of clinical disorders of diverse causes and outcomes; similarly, in this century, the term "childhood schizophrenia" has been applied to children who differ widely in clinical features and course. Progress in the field of mental deficiency has resulted from cumulative success in distinguishing one syndrome from another, in identifying the underlying pathophysiology of many and in devising measures for prevention and treatment based on the discovery of causes. In relation to childhood psychosis, we are at the beginning of an era of systematic investigation which will enable us to separate out subtypes as crucial steps in the search for causes and treatments. In this process, meticulous observation of the longitudinal course of well-characterized groups of psychotic children is an essential part of the clinical method.

The monograph by Dr. Goldfarb and his colleagues on "Psychotic Children Grown Up" is a major contribution to that task. It is a significant addition to the still limited number of reports on the long term outcome of childhood psychosis; it surpasses most in sample size, continuity of observation and duration of follow-up. More importantly, it is unique in describing a group of children who have not only been evaluated but treated for an extended period in an integrated residential

*Dr. Eisenberg is the Maude and Lillian Presley Professor of Psychiatry at the Harvard Medical School and a Senior Associate in Psychiatry at the Children's Hospital Medical Center, Boston, Mass. 02115

Issues in Child Mental Health Vol. 5(2)Spring/Summer, 1978   173
0362-403X/78/1300-0173$00.95 C 1978 Human Sciences Press

treatment center and then have been followed closely into young adulthood. In consequence, the present study provided an unusual opportunity to compare psychiatric status at the termination of the residential treatment program, when the children were about 11, with their status some nine years later. Strikingly, whereas only about a quarter of the children had shown substantial improvement by the end of treatment, another quarter showed significant gains by the end of the follow-up period, whereas very few lost what they had gained. These data provide grounds for greater optimism about the long term prognosis of childhood psychosis than had been warranted by the information heretofore available and pose the question of "sleeper" benefits following intensive treatment.

It is not possible to do justice to all of the important issues raised by this monograph; I will limit my comments to a few: classification, the role of "organic" factors, the evaluation of treatment effects and the unexpected finding of improvement in adolescence.

Terminology in child psychiatry is unsatisfactory in general; confusion is most evident in the nomenclature for childhood psychosis. Such terms as: atypical child, infantile autism, childhood schizophrenia (sometimes divided into subtypes), dementia infantilis, symbiotic psychosis and still others, are in use, often in an idiosyncratic fashion without specification of the criteria for inclusion or exclusion from the category. When Professor Leo Kanner first differentiated "autistic disturbances of affective contact" (Kanner, 1943), he distinguished the novel syndrome he was describing from feeblemindedness, on the one hand, and schizophrenia, on the other. It was to be discriminated from the former by evidence of "good cognitive potentialities" as manifested by "strikingly intelligent physiognomies," excellent rote memory and good performance on the Seguin formboard; it was separable from the latter because "even in cases with the earliest recorded onset of schizophrenia . . . the first observable manifestations were preceded by at least two years of essentially average development" followed by "a more or less *gradual* change in the patients' behavior." He concluded: "We must, then, assume that these children have come into the world with an innate inability to form the usual, biologically provided affective contact with people, just as other children come into the world with innate physical or intellectual handicaps."

It had been Dr. Kanner's practice to exclude children with ascertainable brain disease from the category of early infantile autism. However, others have used the term for children who exhibit the clinical features of autism, whether or not there is coexisting evidence for other disorders of brain function, as, for example, in children with congenital rubella (Chess, 1971). The difficulty in maintaining a clinical basis for the conceptual distinction lies in the uncertain grounds on which the clinician must judge that an autistic child *does* have "good cognitive potentialities" or does *not* have underlying brain disease, even though localizing neurological signs are absent. Indeed, if one recalls Dr. Kanner's initial formulation that "these children have come into the world with an innate inability," this can only be interpreted to mean cerebral malfunction, not otherwise specifiable. Indeed, with the realization that a number of the children who exhibited no obvious neurological abnormality at the time of initial examination went on to display seizures at a later age (Rutter, Greenfield, & Lockyer, 1967), the distinction becomes even more difficult to sustain. Thus, it has become evident that the diagnosis of psychosis in early childhood must be based on clinical psychiatric criteria as described by Kanner (1943) or by the British Working Party (Creak, 1961) and not on presumptions about etiology. Insofar as brain abnormalities can be identified by neurodiagnostic methods (Hauser, DeLong, & Rossman, 1975), these should be specified on an additional axis of classification (Rutter, Lebovici, Eisenberg, Sneznevski, Sadoun, Brooke, & Lin, 1969) in order to permit the neurological data to be taken into account in comparing and contrasting treatment outcome.

On the other hand, I, along with many colleagues, continue to be persuaded that the distinction between the schizophrenias in childhood and the other psychoses of early onset remains important because of the striking differences in clinical manifestations and long term course; in my experience, children with autism do *not* go on to develop clinical features of schizophrenia.

The W.H.O. Seminar on Diagnosis in Child Psychiatry (Rutter et al 1969) proposed the subdivision of psychotic disorders in childhood into: (a) *infantile psychosis*—onset within the first two years and at the latest by the 30th month of life; (b) *disintegrative psychosis*—cases in which normal or near normal development in the first few years is followed by deterioration in affective, cognitive and behavioral development; and (c) *schizophrenia*—a clinical disorder resembling the adult form, with onset in the later years of childhood. Kolvin's data from Newcastle (Kolvin, 1971, pp. 7-26) lend empirical support to the concept on epidemiological grounds because of the bimodal distribution of cases by age of onset. The importance of the clinical distinction is reinforced by differences in course; the disintegrative psychoses uniformly demonstrate a progressively deteriorating course and inevitably require institutionalization; the childhood schizophrenics not only exhibit remissions and exacerbations but may also respond dramatically to psychotropic medication. It would be absurd to argue that diagnosis by age of onset represents a final or a rigid criterion. Schizophrenia can occasionally, if only rarely, be seen before the age of 6 or 7 and disintegrative psychosis (almost certainly a catchall category which includes a variety of degenerative brain diseases) can begin before 3 as well as after 7.

From the standpoint of the W.H.O. criteria, the cases described by Dr. Goldfarb and his colleagues correspond to the category of infantile psychosis. Since infantile psychosis is but one, though the largest, subgroup of childhood psychosis, the use of the latter term in the Ittleson report may result in some confounding when comparisons are made with other studies which include patients not represented in this population. Moreover, the Ittleson sample is a bit narrower than the category of infantile psychosis as used by others because of the employment of an exclusion criterion: the "absence of known and manifest localizing signs of sensory and motor dysfunction and epilepsy." I do not quarrel with the restriction; indeed, it corresponds more closely to Kanner's definition than that employed by the W.H.O. I emphasize the point primarily to delineate the characteristics of the children who have been treated and followed in this study; namely, children with early onset and without "known" brain disease.

This is particularly noteworthy in view of the practice at Ittleson of distinguishing between "organic" children and "nonorganic" children. (It requires considerable self-restraint on my part to avoid a long disquisition on the linguistic absurdity implicit in this awkward terminology; what in heaven's name is a "nonorganic" child, one who is made of pure ectoplasm? I know that Dr. Goldfarb means to distinguish between children with and without nonlocalizing neurological abnormalities, but I wish he had employed more felicitous terms!) The point to be emphasized is that the "organic" cases in this series are very different from the cases with known neurologic disease included by other writers.

Nonetheless, most of us expected, and nodded sagely at, the earlier reports from Ittleson that psychotic children with nonspecific neurological disabilities did less well during residential treatment than those who appeared to be neurologically intact. What shatters complacency are the data from this follow-up study, data which indicate relatively little difference between the outcome in late adolescence for the two groups. The change between short term and long term outcome is accounted for by the larger number of the "organic" cases who showed improvement during the eight years of the follow-up period. However, once the total sample is divided into "organic" and "nonorganic" subgroups, restrictions in sample size make it difficult to draw firm conclusions about post-treatment differences.

Nonetheless, the unexpected finding is the discovery that, whereas about a quarter of the children had shown substantial improvement by the end of the four year period of treatment, another quarter went on to do so within the next eight years. Thus, almost half the cases were in the mildly impaired or normal categories by young adulthood. In a survey of the literature in the English language between 1943 and 1963 (Eisenberg, 1967, p. 1437), I found that the average rate of improvement for the 502 cases described during that period was about 25%, although it is equally noteworthy that it varied from a low of 14% to a high of 36%. Since both the worst (Szurek, 1956) and the best (Brown, 1963) outcomes were reportedly by centers employing intensive psychoanalytic treatment methods, it seems most likely that the variation in outcome reflected differences in inclusion criteria and in sampling bias rather than in the efficacy of treatment. Since that time (excluding earlier reports on the present series by the Ittleson group), there have been four other substantial outcome studies. Fair or good outcome was reported for 40% of the cases in Rutter's (1967) follow-up of 63 children, for 26% of the cases in DeMyer's (DeMyer & Steele, 1973) study of 126 children and for 38% of the cases in Lotter's (1974) study of 29 cases. The one published study which differs markedly from all others in the literature is that by Bettelheim (1967) who reported improvement in 32 of the 40 children he treated. Unfortunately, it is not possible to compare this study directly with the others because, though selected case reports are included, there is no characterization of the total sample. The most parsimonious explanation of the discrepancy between the highly favorable outcome in this series and the others with which it can be compared is a difference in intake criteria. All of the studies, in which outcome has been related to initial level of verbal ability, I.Q. test score or ego function, have shown a substantial correlation between initial assessment and final psychological attainment. Selection for children high on these attributes, whether deliberate or inadverdent, would markedly increase the likelihood of a favorable outcome, without respect to the type of therapeutic intervention.

From this perspective, the outcome at follow-up for the Ittleson series compares favorably with the available data for cases of infantile psychosis. The improvement rate in the present group of cases (49%) is not significantly different from that reported by Rutter (40%), Lotter (38%) or Brown (36%); on the other hand, the outcome is almost twice as good as that reported for the "natural history" of the children evaluated at Hopkins (27%), a few of whom were exposed to intensive treatment programs (Eisenberg, 1956).

This brings us to the most difficult problem of all: evaluating the effectiveness of psychiatric treatment for infantile psychosis. In view of the severity of the disorder and the enormous problems these youngsters present to their parents and to the community, it would neither be ethical nor possible to design a rigorous study which included an untreated control group. Efforts to evaluate treatment outcome can only proceed by comparing the results from a new and hopefully better method with those obtained by the best alternative intervention taken as a base line. Though it would be desirable to compare the two treatment programs concurrently, that ideal may simply not be practicable. Putting together the resources for an innovative therapeutic program will tax the capacities of any medical center; assembling a second program, while continuing to provide the first, may well be impossible. It is likely, therefore, to be necessary to rely on a less satisfactory design; namely, comparing the results of the novel therapy with a historical "control" based upon the results reported in the literature, after having taken as much care as possible to make the new sample comparable to the old one.

It cannot be emphasized too forcefully that the initial characteristics of the group of children selected for treatment will be a major determinent of outcome. From that point of view, the meticulous care with which Dr. Goldfarb and his colleagues have described their patient population provides an invaluable base line. Their discovery of substantial improvement in some children after discharge cautions us once again that assessment of outcome requires long term follow-up. That is both the virtue of the present monograph and a major reason why studies like it are so rare. It is not only that the Ittleson Center has been fortunate in having as gifted a group of research workers as Bill Goldfarb and his colleagues but it is even more unique in having a chief investigator who has committed himself to a quarter century of continuous work at a single institution. In these days of academic mobility and ever shorter geographic half-lives, this is surely an accomplishment worth celebrating!

What accounts for the improvement in the 19 children who were still seriously impaired at the end of four years of intensive treatment but who were found to be only mildly impaired or within the normal range at follow-up eight years later? Does the late improvement represent a "sleeper effect" from the earlier treatment, benefit from additional interventions after discharge, or no more than a manifestation of the vicissitudes of the natural history of the illness? That unexpected improvement in the absence of formal psychiatric treatment can occur is evident from the history of one of Dr. Kanner's original eleven cases (Kanner, 1973). Similar observations have been made on occasion in the course of other follow-up studies. But for "spontaneous improvement" to have occurred in 19 of the 56 children (34%) who were found to be grossly impaired at the age of 11 seems highly improbable. Either of the first two hypotheses must be invoked and we lack grounds to decide between them.

Thus, it will become of very considerable interest to all of us to learn from Dr. Goldfarb and his co-workers in detail about the children who improved during their adolescence in the hope that review of their course and treatment can offer us clues to guide future efforts. I don't know what the families of those youngsters were told about the prospects for their children at the time of their discharge from Ittleson. I am afraid that, had I been the clinician, I would have felt bound to give them a gloomy prognosis on the basis of what my experience had been and what had been reported by others before 1970. What troubles me is not that my expectations have been proved wrong; it is invariably a relief to learn that pessimism is no longer warranted. What is troubling is the realization that I might have recommended inappropriate placement or have discouraged continuing efforts for children who almost certainly would not have done as well had they been regarded as beyond any likely redemption.

All child psychiatrists will await with keen interest the next article in this series from the Henry Ittleson Center, one that we hope will describe the characteristics of the children and the care offered them in such fashion as to enable us to enhance the likelihood of further development in children with infantile psychosis.

REFERENCES

Bettelheim, B. *The empty fortress*. New York: Free Press, 1967.
Brown, J. Follow-up of children with atypical development. *American Journal of Orthopsychiatry*, 1963, *33*, 855-861.
Chess, S. Autism in children with congenital rubella. *Journal of Autism and Childhood Schizophrenia*, 1971, *1*, 33-47.
Creak, M. Schizophrenic syndrome in childhood. *Cerebral Palsy Bulletin*, 1961, *3*, 501.
DeMyer, M.K. & Steele, R. Prognosis in autism: A follow-up study. *Journal of Autism and Childhood Schizophrenia*, 1973, *3*, 199-246.
Eisenberg, L. Autistic children in adolescence. *American Journal of Psychiatry*, 1956, *112*, 607-612.
Eisenberg, L. Psychotic disorders of childhood. In A.M. Freedman & H. Kaplan (Eds.), *Comprehensive textbook of psychiatry*. Baltimore: Williams & Wilkins, 1967.
Hauser, S.L., DeLong, G.R., & Rossman, N.P. Pneumographic findings in the infantile autism syndrome: A correlation with temporal lobe disease. *Brain*, 1975, *98*, 667-688.

Kanner, L. Autistic disturbances of affective contact. *The Nervous Child*, 1943, *2*, 217-250.

Kanner, L. *Childhood psychosis: Initial studies and new insights*. Washington: V.H. Winston and Sons, 1973.

Kolvin, I. Psychoses in childhood - a comparative study. In M. Rutter (Ed.), *Infantile autism: Concepts, characteristics and treatment*. London: Churchill Livingstone, 1971.

Lotter, V. Social adjustment and placement of autistic children in Middlesex: A follow-up study. *Journal of Autism and Childhood Schizophrenia*, 1974, *4*, 11-32.

Rutter, M., Greenfield, D., & Lockyer, L. A five to fifteen year follow-up study of infantile psychosis. II Social and behavioral outcome. *British Journal of Psychiatry*, 1967, *113*, 1183-1199.

Rutter, M., Lebovici, S., Eisenberg, L., Sneznevskij, A.V., Sadoun, R., Brooke, E., & Lin, T.Y. A triaxial classification of mental disorders in childhood. *Journal of Child Psychology and Psychiatry*, 1969, *10*, 41-61.

Szurek, S.A. Psychotic episodes and psychiatric maldevelopment. *American Journal of Orthopsychiatry*, 1956, *26*, 519-543.

INDEX

Abnormal behavior criteria,
114
Abnormal perceptual experi-
ence criteria, 114
Adaptive capacity, 111
Adaptive competence of child,
142-152
Adaptive functioning, quanti-
tative variations, 106
Age of admission, 157-159
Anthony, E. James, 105-107
Anxiety criteria, 114
Autism, 115, 116, 174-175
Autistic children study
(1956), 109-110
Autistic disturbances of affec-
tive contact, 174

Bellak, Leopold, 106

Change and social outcomes,
appraisals of, 122-125
Children, intake criteria,
115-159
    adaptive competence of
    child, 142-152

age of admission to resi-
    dential treatment,
    157-159
appraisals of change and
    social outcomes, 122-125
discussion, 163-170
Ego Status Scale, 120-
    121, 122
factors associated with
    outcome, 133-134
intelligence test ratings,
    122
longitudinal patterns of
    change, 126-133
neurological integrity,
    134-139
race and religion, 119
sex, 152-157
sex and neurological
    status, 120
socio-economic position,
    119, 139-142
statistical treatment, 126
summary of findings,
    159-163
Communication levels, 110

Congenital rubella, 175

Dementia infantilis, 174
Difficulty in mixing criteria,
   114
Diagnostic criteria, 113-115
Disintegrative psychosis, 175
Distortion in motility pat-
   terns, 115

Educational and therapeutic
   influences, 111
Ego status, 110-111
   longitudinal change,
      126-133
   scale for psychiatric ap-
      praisal (in adoles-
      cence), 124-125
Ego status at admission, summary of findings, 162-163
Ego Status at discharge, summary of findings, 163
Ego Status Scale, 120-121,
   122, 123
Ehrmann Foundation, 107,
   108
Eisenberg, Leon, 173-180
Emotional relationships criteria, 114

Feeblemindedness, 174
   global "diagnosis" of
      (19th century), 173
Fisher Exact Probability and
   Chi square tests, 126
Florsheim, Judy, 108-172
Follow-up studies (of psychotic children growing up),
   108-172
   diagnosis of early child-
      hood psychosis, 113-
      115

discussion, 163-170
intake criteria, 115-159
introduction to, 105-107
objectives of present re-
   port, 112-113
summary of findings,
   159-163
See also Infantile psychosis, Outcome of

Goldfarb, Nathan, 108-172
Goldfarb, William, 107, 108-
   172
Hippocratic precept, 105
Hollingshead-Redlich Index of
   Social Position, 118, 139
Hyperkinesis, 115

Infantile psychosis, outcome
   of, 173-180
   evaluating post-treatment
      effects, 177-179
   feeblemindedness diagno-
      sis, 173
   "organic" and "nonor-
      ganic" children, 176-
      177
   "sleeper" benefits fol-
      lowing intensive treat-
      ment, 174, 178
   terminology in child psy-
      chiatry, 174-175
   W.H.O. Seminar, 175-176
Intake criteria, early childhood psychosis, 115-159
   specific practices, 116-
      117
   summary of findings,
      159-163
   See also Children, intake
      criteria
Ittleson Foundation, 107, 108

Kanner, Leo, 174, 175, 179

Lack of integration criteria, 114
Longitudinal patterns of change, 126-133

Meyers, Donald I., 107, 108-172
Mildly impaired:
    defined, 121
    scale for psychiatric appraisal, 124-125
Moderately impaired:
    defined, 121
    scale for psychiatric appraisal, 124-125

National Institute of Mental Health, 107, 108
Neurological integrity, 134-139
    summary of findings, 162
Normal:
    defined, 121
    scale for psychiatric appraisal, 124-125

"Organic" and "nonorganic" children, distinguishing between, 176-177

Pathological preoccupation with objects, 114
Playing with other children criteria, 114
"Poor premorbidity," 170

Residential programs, 111-112
Residential treatment, age of admission to, 157-159

Resistance to change criteria, 114
Retardation, 115

Schizophrenia, 113-114, 115, 164, 169
Seguin formboard, 174
Self-directed aggression criteria, 114
Severely impaired:
    defined, 121
    scale for psychiatric appraisal, 124,125
Sex, intake criteria, 152-157
Sex, role of, 110-111
Sex, summary of findings, 163
"Sleeper effect," 174,178
Socio-economic position, 111, 139-142
    intake criteria, 119
    summary of findings, 162
Speech criteria, 115
Speech level, 110
Statistical treatment, 126
Symbiotic psychosis, 114, 174

Unawareness of personal identity criteria, 114

Very severely impaired:
    defined, 121
    scale for psychiatric appraisal, 124-125

Wechsler Intelligence Scale for Children, 122; See also Adaptive competence of children
W.H.O. Seminar on Diagnosis in Child Psychiatry, 175-176
William T. Grant Foundation, 107, 108